LeadershipFlow
PERFECTLY
SQUARE

LeadershipFlow Perfectly Square

Published by Clovercroft Publishing, Franklin, Tennessee.

Cover Design by Marika Van Adelsberg @The Story Studio

Interior Design by iMAGiNE Communications

Edited by Bob Burris, Lesley McCreath @The Story Studio

Printed in the United States of America

978-1-945507-49-6

LeadershipFlow
PERFECTLY
SQUARE

A Story About Learning to Lead and Transforming a Company

Croft Edwards

Clovercroft/Publishing

Dedication

For Nan and Ralph—who planted in me
the seed of leadership

For Dad—thanks for the gift of woodworking

For Jeanne, Sophie, Olivia, and Ana—
my loves and my greatest joys!

Acknowledgments

It is with gratitude and humility that I wish to thank all of those who helped to bring this book to fruition:

To the wise and wonderful Emily Aiken and all of her team @The Story Studio. Your wisdom and gifts have brought this book alive. Emily, you truly are a genius and I cannot thank you enough. To Bob Burris, an editor with an ear for a great story, your additions make the story come alive. Lesley McCreath, thanks for your editing and grammatical guidance in all my writing, while at the same time allowing my voice to remain.

To all my teachers, especially those in the Ontological/Generative discourse—Julio Olalla, thanks for opening this discourse for me and for thousands of others. Bob Dunham, thank you for teaching me to see organizations on a cellular level. I honor your wisdom. Richard Strozzi-Heckler for showing me how to truly show up as a man and as a leader. To all my fellow coaches, thanks for your support and coaching along the way. To Terrie Lupberger, Dave Hasenbalg, Bob Dunham, and Margie Newlin, a special thanks to you for providing your insights during the editing process. To my wife, Jeanne, thanks for years of being an ear to listen and taking the time to be my wise editing partner—I love you.

My path to learning about leadership was blessed with many clients who, through sharing their leadership challenges, allowed me to learn in their laboratory. To each, thanks for your trust in me; I hope it was time well spent for you. Specifically, Lynn Keddington, thank you for trusting me when others did not; Mike Wright, thank you for continuing that trust, and Rex Kontz, for teaching me through your wisdom and modeling of leadership.

Finally to my family, I honor all of you and thank you for allowing me to chase my dreams. You paved the way and supported me in my journey. I love you all.

Contents

Foreword
by Ted Coine

I first met Croft through our interactions on social media. We instantly hit it off and as we grew closer, shared many enlightening conversations about leadership and leading in the age of social media. There is no shortage of leadership gurus and experts out there, but from the very beginning I saw that Croft had a fresh, vital, and highly actionable take on leadership. Others focus on the traits of leaders, building trust, integrity, purpose, and the like—all great stuff—but ultimately leading to the same questions: How do you build those things? Can you actually learn how to lead with integrity? How does one truly inspire trust?

Croft provides clear answers to these essential questions. He opened up a world for me that demonstrated how a person can embody leadership—and how the conversations leaders and teams have, and the moods and emotions people bring to the table, provide the foundation for all that is to follow. Furthermore, he showed me that all of these things are learnable and teachable—and if done effectively, can inspire a visceral response within an organization, one that is about tapping Flow, that state of performance where everyone is at their best. These were powerful insights for me and opened my eyes to seeing leadership like I never had before.

Best of all, Croft is a great communicator, a wonderful storyteller—a man who makes learning accessible, informative, and fun. As I read this book I found that the story itself was entertaining and enriching, a great read apart from the important principles it has to impart. With the added layer of Croft's insights and lessons, well, it is truly something special.

I believe you'll appreciate the journey and the growth every bit as much as I have. So enjoy the story and be open to learning about how to become a truly great leader.

Ted Coine

Co-Author, *A World Gone Social*, and Social Media Influencer

Preface

I have a confession to make. I am an addict, although I did not know this until about three years ago. In the process of rebranding my company, my amazing branding partner, Emily Aiken, and I were exploring how I approached things. What I thought was ordinary behavior, Emily helped me to see as a link I had been missing in my search for understanding leadership. Emily observed that in my everyday life I was searching for Flow. I did it in my woodshop when I was building furniture. I did it on long runs as I trained for marathons. I did it when I was exploring the study of leadership. I was addicted to Flow—that state of ultimate performance when I was at my best and felt my best. It was in Flow when I got so immersed in a woodworking project that I could hear the wood telling me how to cut it and lost all track of time, when I'd run five miles and it felt like only five minutes had passed, when I identified the qualities that great leaders seem to almost instinctively embody. Flow brings out the best in individuals, and for me I realized I was constantly seeking that natural high of being my best.

As I jumped into the study of Flow I discovered it was the missing link in effective leadership. Instead of reaching for goals or a mission, reaching for Flow is at the heart of dynamic leadership. Flow in one's self as a leader, Flow in one's teammates, and employees. Flow in the organization. If everyone could find Flow on a more regular basis, then the organization could easily surpass its previous levels of performance. Flow is about optimal performance; it is the job of the leader to find Flow.

This was profound for me. I could now take my deep and long-term study of leadership and see clearly what a leader should be working toward. I really started to understand how, in the conversations of leadership, the leader is trying to get the performer to be committed to what he or she is doing, not just be compliant. It became more and more clear that we follow leaders who bring out the Flow in us.

Here now is a story to share with you about how to bring Flow alive through generative leadership distinctions. Here is the story of one leader's journey to find LeadershipFlow.

Staff Meeting

It was the usual 7:30 a.m. Tuesday staff meeting at the Albuquerque office of Perfectly Square, a successful woodworking supply store. Representatives from the Phoenix, Denver, and Tucson branches of the company weighed in on the speakerphone as e-commerce and warehouse manager Cynthia Hernandez, store manager Jason Shumway, the lead in-store sales person Marty Thompson, and other employees of the Albuquerque office took notes and drank their morning coffee. Mark Andrews, the youthful CEO of the company, ran the meeting from his usual spot at the head of the employee-built quartersawn white oak Mission table. Jacqueline "Jackie" Andrews, the newest member of the team, sat at her brother's right hand, her focus and air of confidence belying her status as a newcomer. For Jackie, the meeting was a homecoming of sorts; she was joining the family business for the first time since she had worked various jobs in the warehouse and showroom throughout high school.

Mark sat at the head of the table, because when his father was alive and running the business that is what he did. Mark did it out of default, not because he felt like the leader of the company, but because he really did not know what else to do but try to emulate his father. This meeting was like that of any other Tuesday morning, parsing over hot issues and routine mundane matters that usually were never really resolved, just discussed and then tucked away for another week. Today's meeting ventured into a slow-burning fire that needed to be put out (or at least discussed): the fact that Perfectly Square was taking longer than its stated goal of shipping orders within twenty-four hours. This issue was becoming more and more common in the meetings; however, no one ever really owned it and instead the talk digressed to finger pointing and blame-avoidance, often with the vague aura of personal attack.

"I don't understand why we continue to have this issue," Mark said halfheartedly to Cynthia.

Cynthia tensely rolled a pencil between her thumb and forefinger. "We're doing all we can, but every time I go to the other departments to sort things out, I have trouble finding anyone or I run into the TableSaw Mafia on one of their many coffee breaks." Cynthia didn't need to call out Jason and Marty by name. Everyone knew she was referring to the two de-facto leaders of the group of long-time employees whose primary task seemed to be to try to stop change and growth within the company.

"Don't blame us, we have all of our sales going out the door and we hit our numbers," Marty said without any hint of apology or explanation, almost as if to say that Cynthia had no relevance to his place in the organization.

Jason was more direct. "Look, this issue has been building for a long time; maybe it needs to be addressed at the root of the problem." He looked directly at Cynthia, placing the blame squarely on her. "I'm not about to jeopardize my future because of the inability of others to get their jobs done."

"Enough," Mark sighed. "We've got to figure this out

before our e-commerce and reputation start to tank. Any ideas?"

Behind her placid expression, Jackie's mind was racing from the panic of, "Oh shit, what did I get myself into?" to feeling sympathy for Cynthia because of the unvarnished attacks on her from the more senior members of the organization. What was really palpable to her was the fact that the organization appeared to be adrift. Mark was physically present, but it seemed like he didn't want to be working for the family business at all, let alone be the leader. She knew full well that she was going to have to deal with her emotions because she was all in. She had come home to help the business survive, and she knew that at some point, she was going to have to get off the sidelines and join the fray … unfortunately, she was not even sure where to begin.

Jackie Andrews

Jackie was the younger of the two Andrews kids. Her parents, Fred and Mary, were high school sweethearts and had stuck together through thick and thin. Fred was drafted right out of high school and sent off to Vietnam, where fortunately, he served in relatively safe Saigon for the duration of his time in the country. When he returned home, he and Mary married and settled down, and Fred went to work for his father's lumber supply company while somehow managing to earn his business degree by burning the midnight oil, weekends included. By the time Jackie was born, Fred had transformed the company into one of the most successful woodworking supply companies in the United States.

Jackie lived an idyllic childhood, until she was about fifteen. The success of Perfectly Square meant Mary could stay home and raise the kids; and as Fred was CEO, he could easily make time to be actively involved in his children's upbringing. When Jackie was a sophomore in high school, her mother died after a short battle with cancer. Jackie funneled her grief into an assortment of activities that over time became increasingly athletic in nature. She competed in cross-country and basketball, and when she wasn't studying she worked at Perfectly Square doing whatever odd jobs her father found for her. Her exemplary athletic and academic performance afforded Jackie her choice of top colleges, and she eventually chose Michigan State on an Air Force ROTC scholarship.

As with all she did, Jackie excelled in ROTC and her studies, earning a BA degree in Finance. By her senior year, she was the cadet Battalion Commander and commissioned a Second Lieutenant in the Air Force for a five-year commitment. Jackie loved the Air Force as it allowed her to see the world as a Personnel Officer both stateside and during a three-year tour in Germany. She kept very busy on active duty touring Europe and finishing her MBA through a distance program—all while earning excellent performance marks as an Air Force officer.

Life was good until the horrible night she received the call that her father had died unexpectedly of a heart attack. Facing overwhelming grief for the second time, Jackie felt a powerful need to come home, be with her brother, and help out with the family business, but still had her five-year commitment to the Air Force, which she fulfilled. She was given leave to come home for the funeral, but never got the chance to really talk to Mark before having to return overseas.

After two years of amiable but somewhat perfunctory conversations with Mark, which never touched on the future of the company, Jackie finally was able to leave the Air Force and come home to join the business. Although her decision was primarily fueled by the desire to help the family business, she couldn't deny the spark of ambition within her that viewed joining the company as exciting a challenge as she'd ever faced. That spark would be critically challenged as she began her journey.

It was not entirely clear what role Jackie would have with the company. She and Mark had never had anything resembling that conversation, but the clearest path forward seemed to be for her to spend a year or so learning various functions of the company and then as her knowledge evolved, she and Mark would determine the position from which she could best help. During that year, she had the luxury of being an owner of the company and would be able to influence people until she had an official job.

The Albuquerque Store

Without a clear direction, and sensing the confusion in her first staff meeting, Jackie decided to spend her first day on the floor in the Albuquerque store, something she thought she should do for two or three months before moving on to other departments. She wanted to learn the reality of Perfectly Square from the ground up and take the time necessary to do so properly. The showroom was practically deserted when she arrived at the store a little after 8:30 a.m., as it didn't open until 10:00 a.m. Shouldering her laptop bag and still clutching a Styrofoam cup of coffee from the staff meeting, she found a small cubicle in the back offices to serve as her temporary home and started on routine tasks such as logging on to the Wi-Fi (she finally found the password on a scrap of paper taped inside the desk drawer) and answering emails.

About 9:00 a.m. Jason Shumway, whom she'd known since she was a kid, stuck his head in. Jason had been with the company for nearly twenty-four years, starting soon after graduation from high school, and had worked hard to become the branch manager. He'd gone to night school and earned an associate degree in business from nearby Central New Mexico Community College. Jason had worked nearly every job in the store and warehouse, and was one of Fred's favorites. He had been the store manager for only a few years when Fred died, and although he knew he was a bit under-qualified to take over as CEO, he was not happy when Mark was handed the reins. He tolerated Mark, but deep down believed Mark was a bit of a silver spoon child and felt, as many did, that Mark was not really qualified to take over the company and did not really relish being CEO.

"Hello and welcome aboard. You ready to learn how this plane flies?" Jason asked.

"A bit overwhelmed but ready to jump in. Where do we start?"

"You tell me, you are sort of the boss," Jason said with a twinge of cynicism.

"I wouldn't go that far," Jackie replied, "I'm just hoping to drink from the proverbial fire hose to figure out how I can help best. But since you ask, why don't you just do what you do every day and I'll be a fly on the wall. A fly that occasionally asks questions, that is."

Jason didn't react to the joke. "I have a daily kick-off meeting at nine-thirty with the store personnel; why don't you join me out on the floor around then and we'll take it from there?"

"Great, see you then."

The 9:30 a.m. kick-off meeting started about 9:35 with a huddle of the meager sales staff along with Cynthia Hernandez, whom Jackie knew before she was the e-commerce and warehouse manager. Jackie later learned that Cynthia usually joined the morning meeting to check in and attempt to build bridges with the store team.

Jason started off the meeting by going over some housekeeping. "I'm also going to need somebody to volunteer to help with the ongoing backlog in the warehouse with the e-commerce shipping."

Jason looked around as most of the sales team sheepishly averted their eyes. They were on a salary plus commission pay system and, out of financial self preservation, weren't about to step forward and do extra work that would cost them potential earnings. Perhaps equally important, there was little love lost between the sales staff and the warehouse; most of the sales people believed the company would be better off without e-commerce as it did not seem to really add much value and frequently created uncomfortable situations like this.

After what seemed like minutes Patrick Lee, one of the relatively new and younger sales staff, gave a defeated sigh. "I'll do it."

Everyone gave their own sighs of relief—Cynthia because she liked Patrick's gung-ho attitude, and the other sales people because Patrick's hustle on the floor usually translated into less commission for them.

"That's good; thanks, Patrick, now the old timers can make more sales," Jason said, almost flippantly.

Some of the others laughed and the meeting wrapped up as people prepared the store for opening. Jackie watched as Cynthia and Patrick headed back to the warehouse to start unraveling the shipping mess. Although she wanted to go with them, she'd committed to spending the first few months with Jason in the store and decided to stick with the plan, at least for today.

Later that morning, Jason showed Jackie how they tracked sales and the challenges of the shipping backlog. "A lot of the issues we face with the warehouse are not tied to the computer system; really they're more like personnel problems." He lowered his voice conspiratorially. "Not to slam your brother, but if he would deal with Cynthia a lot of the issues would disappear."

"Why do you think Cynthia is the issue?" Jackie asked.

It was clear Jason had been waiting to unload on Cynthia to anyone with a semblance of authority. "She creates a lot of the drama by always claiming she is understaffed and then turns around and blames the system. Mark listens to her but never does anything about it. Between you and me, she's a problem and rather than solving it, Mark keeps fueling it."

"Have you guys tried to help out the warehouse?"

Jason gave an involuntary snort. "Please—we have to look out for ourselves. We don't have time to focus on her issues, plus if we did, in-store sales would suffer. My guys keep this place afloat." Somehow he managed to make the words sound both pleading and condescending, as if to imply that his team was beyond Jackie's ability to control.

Jackie was about to ask a follow-up question when Jason's attention went to a customer entering the store. "I need to take care of something," he said brusquely and hurried off with a friendly smile to meet the customer.

Jackie spent the rest of the day shadowing Jason. She noted that he seemed to have a good rapport with most of the team, except for those in the warehouse and e-commerce area. She observed that his interactions with the customers were always pleasant, though with some it seemed almost too friendly. On several occasions she watched with interest as he threw an arm around a buyer's shoulder and walked him out to the parking lot for what appeared to be a private conversation. Jackie filed her observations away, and for the rest of the week worked with Jason, learning sales and getting grounded in the store's operation. It seemed to be busy, which was good—but something about it all didn't sit well with Jackie. At this point it was nothing she could put into words, but neither could she ignore the creeping uneasiness in her body.

Jim Catlett

During her second week in the showroom, a familiar face brightened Jackie's day.

"Uncle Jim!" Jackie beamed, giving the sturdy and fit older man a big hug. "It's so good to see you!"

"Welcome, or should I say welcome back," he said, a warm twinkle in his eye. "From high school helper to Air Force Officer, to now some kind of owner around here, I guess. I bet you're excited to be back."

Jackie flashed a nervous smile. "Excited, scared, and a tiny bit ready to go back to my old job."

Jim Catlett was an interesting man, one who'd been part of Jackie's life for as long as she could remember. He had grown up in Albuquerque and was her father's best friend, finding innocent trouble wherever they went. They both went into the military, but while Fred was drafted and sent to Vietnam, Jim went to college and joined Army ROTC. He loved the Army, both the physical and leadership challenges it presented. At each level Jim stood out from his peers. He commanded an armor battalion in Operation Desert Storm, earning a commendation for his leadership. He ended up commanding a Brigade and possibly could have made General had he not decided to retire after twenty- eight years because of his wife's failing health and his desire to enjoy life with her.

The one thing Jim loved almost as much as his wife and the Army was woodworking. Most Army bases had a full wood shop for soldiers to use, and Jim immediately took to it, quickly building the mastery that he did in so many aspects of his life. The only problem with his new-found passion was that when he retired, he no longer had access to a wood shop. When he moved back to Albu-querque and reconnected with Fred and their families, a solution to his problem became apparent. Jim's interest in woodworking led him to Perfectly Square, where he spent many an afternoon talking with Fred and other old timers about woodworking. Fred offered to help Jim stock his own wood shop with tools at wholesale, but Jim didn't feel right doing that. They agreed to a compromise where Jim would work in the store a few days a week. This was a win for Jim as it allowed him to buy tools and supplies at a great discount, get out a few days a week, and im-merse himself in a woodworking culture. The store also benefitted from Jim's upbeat, positive attitude and deep woodworking knowledge, which quickly endeared him to Perfectly Square's clientele. Jim had finally re-retired a year or so earlier, but still dropped by the store frequently, had a free run of the place, knew all of the players, and of course, still qualified for the family discount.

Despite his leadership and organizational effective-ness experience, Jim did not get involved much with the running of the business. When Fred was alive, the two talked regularly and Jim served as his friend's sound-ing board and unofficial coach. After Fred died, Mark seemed strangely reluctant to take Jim up on his many offers to help. Jim respected Mark's desire to learn about leadership on his own, but at times it was hard for him to watch a leader who did not really want to be in that role, or know how to lead. However, Jim never allowed it to get in the way of his shopping at the store, and still loved being connected with the business.

"I can't think of anyone else better qualified to take this place into the future than you," said Jim, quickly adding, "along with your brother, that is." Jackie knew Jim well enough to detect his mild endorsement of Mark, but she decided not to press the issue.

'Thanks for the vote of confidence; I may need your help. More than you know," Jackie said, her smile fading a bit.

"Any time," replied Jim.

"Next week, coffee and burritos, on me?"

"Pick the time, and I'm there—but it's on me."

"I'll get back to you on the date; right now I'm up to my ears in e-commerce and warehouse issues."

"Looking forward to it," Jim grinned. "And now I understand there's a new shipment of exotic hardwoods that needs to end up in my wood shop."

Jackie fondly watched Jim head off with his steady gait, unable to resist the thoughts of how much he reminded her of her father and the firm hand he seemed to have on the company and seemingly everything he touched. Would she ever stop missing him? Then, tucking her feelings away, she turned and headed for the warehouse to find out more about what it was that was going wrong.

The Warehouse

Even though Jackie's plan was to spend a few months in the store getting a handle on the retail side of things, it seemed like she was being sucked into a big swamp of quicksand called the warehouse and e-commerce shipping.

Around the turn of the century, Perfectly Square began to embrace the world of e-commerce. Fred had been open to expanding the business and selling products that had done well in online stores. Like most businesses new to e-commerce, Perfectly Square had ups and downs learning how to design and implement a website that could lead to actual sales. The growing pains had proven to be worth it, with e-commerce now accounting for almost half of Perfectly Square's sales volume as well as maintaining a healthy profit margin. From its very inception, Perfectly Square had built its success on customer service. If an order was placed by noon Mountain time, the company did whatever it took to have it shipped the same day, at least within twenty-four hours. This required a constantly improving process to keep pace with the steadily growing orders. Until recently the warehouse and e-commerce team had continued to grow and meet the demands. But lately …

Cynthia Hernandez, a dedicated, hard working, and fairly dynamic leader, had evolved into the leader of the warehouse and e-commerce department. She had started in the warehouse right about the time the company got into Internet sales. As the department grew, Cynthia always seemed to be a step ahead of the change. While working at Perfectly Square she found the time to juggle her job, life as a single mother, and her role as a part-time student, earning her degree in business from The University of New Mexico. Between her competency and her education, she was the obvious choice to run the department. She had paid her dues, was committed to the team, and organization, and truly cared about her job. It was only recently that people had begun to question whether or not she was up to the task. In the last few years, without Fred's guidance, the standards and performance of the e-commerce department had slipped. For the first time ever, orders were taking longer than twenty-four hours to ship, which was why Jackie was pulled in the direction of the warehouse.

As Jackie walked back to the warehouse she ran into Cynthia, who was in the middle of an intense conversation with Jamie Sanders, a key player and the warehouse lead.

"I get that you did not actually see the invoice, but that does not mean we can just act like it doesn't exist or not fulfill the order. Can you please not make a big deal of this and help me?" Cynthia pleaded with Jamie, her face a mix of determination and frustration. As Jackie would learn, it was Jamie's job to physically run the warehouse and its team. Jamie was, for the most part, a solid performer, but at times could be quite dramatic in the process, with his penchant for occasionally playing the role of victim and making mountains out of molehills.

"I am helping you. I just want you to know that if

we don't get the orders or see the invoices we can't fulfill them. We're doing all we can," Jamie replied in frustration.

"Point taken, but we still have to figure this out or it will keep getting worse," Cynthia replied. Jamie nodded and headed back toward the warehouse. Cynthia turned to see that Jackie had overheard the exchange.

"More issues, huh?"

"More of the same would be more accurate," sighed Cynthia.

"What can I do to help?" Jackie asked, not knowing how much help she could be, but throwing a smile in for good measure just in case.

"Could you clone yourself and Jamie times three?" Cynthia asked in frustration.

"Wish I could, but I'm thinking you might not want all the headaches that come with six new employees," Jackie smiled bigger. This time her joke served to ease the tension.

"True, but it would be nice to have some more help," said Cynthia.

"I'm free all afternoon; what can I do?" asked Jackie.

Cynthia eyed a huge desk covered with papers. "I guess we could start over here," she said, leading Jackie over.

"Not exactly the most efficient filing system I've ever seen," Jackie ventured.

"It's more than a bad filing system. It's the control center for the order processing."

Jackie started to laugh until she realized that Cynthia wasn't joking.

The challenges facing the e-commerce team were not unlike those of many organizations experiencing rapid growth; with no strategy in place, they were just reacting rather than figuring out the best way to grow. They had no vision of what success looked like, so they stumbled along through the sloppiest and most inefficient form of evolution.

"We grew out of the warehouse a long time ago." Cynthia's brow furrowed at the mess before her. "We haphazardly added on more space, which was not well planned or thought out. As things continued to grow, we were always too busy and too understaffed to actually re-design how the warehouse is laid out …"

"So there's a lot of waste in energy and walking around trying to efficiently fill orders," Jackie said, completing Cynthia's thought.

Cynthia nodded. "Another challenge is that IT didn't really keep up with the growth either."

This time it was Jackie who nodded. Even though she was relatively new, she was already aware that Perfectly Square's IT department consisted of exactly one person, who spent most of his time simply trying to keep their systems running and who had neither the desire nor skill to really think about the big picture—where the company needed to be to succeed.

"Sometimes we're dealing with physical computer breakdowns or software issues," Cynthia continued, "so we'll jump in and do things manually to get the orders shipped within twenty- four hours—but that means we don't have time to come back and take care of the paperwork. At some point the accountants get involved and then the focus is on catching up and untangling the paper-work, which then challenges the ability to deliver products in a timely matter."

A vicious cycle, Jackie acknowledged, which, with each rotation, undoubtedly leads to resignation and resentment within the team. The future did not look bright at all as something had to give. At the root of it all was a lack of accountability.

As Cynthia continued to explain the never-ending loop of backlog, Jackie began to understand that perhaps Cynthia was not the bad person the team in the store had made her out to be. The more Cynthia talked, the more Jackie picked up on positivity and a can-do attitude that put her at odds with the apathy and negativity spreading through her department.

"I'm willing to step up and own that it's my team and department starting to slip. What frustrates me the most is …" Cynthia nervously chewed her lip, thinking better of what she was about to say.

"You can be completely open with me, Cynthia. I need to know what's going on so I can help fix it."

Cynthia thought for a moment before cautiously proceeding. "I love Mark, but the thing is he doesn't really seem to want to deal with it at all. Whenever I try to raise issues with him, he does all he can to attempt to appease me in the moment … but then when the storm passes, he just goes on to whatever the next issue is."

Or the next issue he wants to avoid, thought Jackie. She knew her brother well and was quite aware of how he dealt with crises—or more accurately, was uneasy dealing with them. When he found himself in an uncomfortable spot, he'd do all he could not to lead or make a decision by disappearing into analysis and data. All his life, his need for obscure information before acting allowed him not to make decisions, which only created more issues. She'd hoped that in the time they'd been apart he had improved in this regard, but was beginning to have her doubts. She loved her brother, but had her suspicions about why the ship was drifting under his command.

"Is there anything else?"

Cynthia looked Jackie in the eye, as if to reassure herself that she could trust Jackie. "I really question at times whether Mark wants to be here. I don't mean 'be here' literally, but it seems to me that he doesn't want to be the CEO."

There was an awkward silence as Jackie processed something that she was starting to see was real. Cynthia wondered if she'd gone too far. When Jackie finally spoke, her relief was palpable.

"That seems like something I should talk to him about. Which I will the next time we have some time," Jackie replied, recognizing that she was venturing into dangerous territory, seeing her brother's lack of commitment to his job, but wanting to remain loyal and support him. Plus, she was starting to make promises that she was not sure she wanted to keep.

Fortunately for Jackie, at that moment Jason popped his head in, creating more havoc for Cynthia by trying to circumvent standard procedures in order to make a sale for the day. This ignited a battle between the two that blazed on for several minutes, for which Jackie had a ringside seat. As they argued, Jackie realized that her desire to remain impartial and take her time to learn the ropes was idealistic and naive.

She was either going to have to show up as a leader or she would become part of the problem.

The First Burrito

Days after her conversation with Cynthia, a thousand competing thoughts and emotions still wrestled for Jackie's attention. Had she gotten herself in over her head? Were the warehouse issues foreshadowing the impending collapse of the company? And the thought currently at the front of the pack—was Mark up to the task of truly leading the company? Yet despite her inner storm, the clouds parted when she ran into Jim, on one of his regular store visits to pick up some white oak for one of his projects.

"Somebody sure looks like they're carrying the weight of the world on their shoulders," said Jim.

"Is it that obvious?" Jackie somehow managed a smile.

"Let's just say I've seen that look on the face of more than one leader with monumental challenges placed at their feet."

"I'm ready to take you up on your offer. I could really use some perspective to help me with—well, with a lot of things," sighed Jackie.

"I'm pretty much booked up today; how's tomorrow morning?"

"Eight a.m., or as you would say, oh-eight-hundred, at the Coffee Shack?"

"Wouldn't miss it. Remember, I'm buying," Jim replied in a way that was far more comforting and reassuring than it had a right to be.

The Coffee Shack was literally around the corner from Perfectly Square, and was therefore a popular place for people from the store to grab coffee or, even better, the mouth-watering amalgamation of eggs, meat, potatoes, and fresh Hatch green chiles wrapped in a steaming tortilla known as the green chile breakfast burrito, a New Mexico staple.

Jackie prided herself on always arriving early for meetings, and today was no exception. She stepped into the inviting, warm aroma of the Coffee Shack at 7:45 a.m. in order to finish collecting her thoughts for the conversation with Jim. She knew he loved green chile burritos, as did she, and of course his coffee—black—just like he had had his entire Army career; she ordered accordingly so that breakfast would be ready when Jim arrived. As she sipped her rich latte—after all she'd never been in the Army, she was in the Air Force—she thought about how to begin. She knew she could trust Jim; in nearly every way he was an uncle to her, plus he knew volumes about leadership and organizations. But where to start?

The challenges in the store with shipping and the e-commerce team? Her concerns about her brother? Was there a way to share that without seeming like she was taking cheap shots, or worse, betraying him? Then there were the lingering questions about Jason Shumway and her unshakeable feeling that something about him was not right. Finally she decided she would just start talking and allow Jim, in his wisdom, to help her figure things out. This was nothing new; Jim had been her counselor and mentor many times before, instrumental in her choosing to go into the Air Force ROTC and advising her at other pivotal points in her career.

Jim entered at 8 a.m. sharp, all of his military bearing

still on display. He saw Jackie, and then the two fresh, hot burritos.

"You didn't have to do that; I said I was going to treat."

"Think of it as my fee for your services as a doctor of leadership," Jackie replied with a disarming smile, which had its intended effect.

"I'll let it slide this time, but next time, it's on me."

"You might want to hear what's on my mind before you start talking about a next time."

The first few bites of burrito were shared with small talk about how Jim's wife was doing and how Jackie was settling back in her hometown. In characteristic style, Jim soon got down to business.

"First and foremost, I want you to know that whatever we talk about stays between us, so you can speak candidly without worrying about where it might go. I know you want what's best for the company, as do I, and that's the position we'll operate from. From there, it's your call whether I'm an ear to listen, a coach to help you, or simply an old friend to have breakfast with. Just let me know how I can help."

"Thanks so much," said Jackie, considering her latte. "Today I thought I could just vent and see what develops from there." As she spoke, the world already seemed a bit brighter.

Jim indicated for her to proceed, and for the next half hour, Jackie took Jim on a tour of her world. She shared her concerns for the company overall. As she saw it, the store had grown faster than the thinking of its leaders, and was now in a place where its success was also dragging it down. She shared her assessments of the strengths and weaknesses of Cynthia, Jason, and even Mark. Through it all, Jim listened attentively, occasionally asking clarifying questions. As Jackie talked, she sensed that things were beginning to become ordered in her own mind, and that alone justified the time they were spending.

When she finished, Jim asked only one question. "How can I help?"

Jackie had to admit she was stumped.

A Place to Start

Seeing Jackie's consternation, Jim leaned forward. "It might help if I start with a story. I took over my battalion about eighteen months before we deployed for the war. I know you're well aware of how well we performed in combat and didn't suffer a single casualty, due primarily to the leadership—top to bottom—in the organization. But when I arrived, we were not a high performing organization. Far from it.

"The previous commander of the organization was a micro- manager who led through fear and intimidation and was relieved of his command because of the toxic environment he'd created. There was a lot of work to do, and I was only given a few weeks to get ready to take over. I'd really been studying leadership because, like all leaders, my primary role was to get the most out of my organization. My first day on the job my new boss, a great leader in his own right who went on to become a four-star general, invited me into his office and outlined his four tenets of leadership, which I've come to call Leadership-Flow."

Jim took a new, clean napkin from the napkin holder on the table, pulled a pen from his pocket, and drew a simple diagram with two circles, and divided the outer circle into thirds. He then wrote, "Creating Culture and Expanding Capacity" in the bottom left of the diagram.

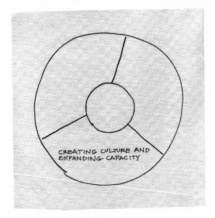

CREATING CULTURE AND EXPANDING CAPACITY

"'Jim,' he said, "'any organization's culture is one-hundred percent perfect in getting the results it is currently getting, so if you want different results from this unit, job one is to change the culture.'"

Jackie listened intently.

"In the same way, the culture of Perfectly Square is one-hundred percent perfect in getting the results it is currently getting."

"So if I'm unhappy, I'll have to change the culture?" Jackie finished his thought. "The million-dollar question then becomes, how?"

"We'll get to that, but right now I want to know your thoughts on the culture of Perfectly Square as it currently stands."

The question blindsided Jackie; it was a perspective she'd never considered. "What exactly do you mean by culture?"

"What did it mean when you were in the Air Force?"

Jackie thought for a moment before responding. "The way we did things. What was expected of us: systems, organizational structure, processes, values, ethics, traditions. Aim High ... Fly-Fight-Win," she smiled with more than a tinge of pride.

"Exactly. In the Army we put it, 'Duty, Honor, Country.' So how do these ideas apply to Perfectly Square?"

"Well, there are elements my father instilled that are still evident—but other elements I'm not sure of. The fact that I can't put my finger on what the culture is, isn't good, is it?"

"I've found there are two things to look at in order to truly understand an organization's culture. First, and this was something I was blind to in the beginning: Everything is a conversation."

"I'm not sure I completely follow ..."

"Neither was I when I first heard it. But let's think about it. The most fundamental tools that humans have are language and the ability to have conversations. The better, the more effective those conversations are, the sooner the point of conversation will become reality. How is it that you and I are here at the Coffee Shack having a delicious burrito?" Jim took his last bite.

"We talked about it and it happened."

"We did more than talk, though; we had an effective conversation. You requested that we have coffee and talk, and I accepted. It is the effectiveness of that conversation that led us here, just as the conversation we are having now is opening up more conversations. We create the future through our conversations: the ones we have effectively, ineffectively, or don't have at all."

Jackie nodded, seeing the truth in his words.

"I have an idea. Let's meet later today at the store and

walk this concept throughout the entire store and warehouse and see what we find."

Jackie found the idea immediately energizing. "I can't wait. But as long as we're here, what about the other tenets?"

Jim regarded her, a twinkle in his eye. "In good time; I don't want to overwhelm you. Let's get to work building on this conversation and as we progress, I'll share with you a way to shift the culture of Perfectly Square. And the best part is we'll have fun while we do it, because, that's the key anyway."

"I like the mystery," said Jackie. "I'm looking forward to this afternoon and our conversations—almost as much as I'm looking forward to you paying for the next breakfast burrito!"

Everything is a Conversation

About one in the afternoon Jim and Jackie met up in the showroom of the store. "Ready to go on walkabout?" he asked her. Walkabout was a term Jim used with his subordinates when he was in command. It was an informal walk around the organization just to observe people in their "natural environment," as Jim liked to say.

"All in; where shall we start?" Jackie asked enthusiastically.

"Remember how I said that everything is a conversation? Well, there are fundamentally three types of conversations: Effective Conversations, Ineffective Conversations, and Missing Conversations. I was thinking we could wait right here and find out which kind we'll come across first." He motioned across the showroom. "Over there by the table saws. What do you see?"

"Patrick Lee talking to that gentleman," replied Jackie, unsure if she was supposed to have noticed something else.

"That is correct, but there is more at play. That gentleman is finally going to buy the new Rocket-Two-Thousand Table Saw he has been eying for about a year."

"How can you know that?"

"Because I recognize an effective conversation when I see one. Most of the other sales people have given up on that customer, but Patrick's been talking to him every time he comes in—and takes his time. For a guy like that, a table saw is a major purchase; he needed to know if Perfectly Square was the place to buy the saw and ultimately, if that was the right saw for him. Patrick has been having conversations with him that have addressed all his needs. That's why he is finally going to buy the saw today. Effective conversations happen when both sides have their cares addressed and get what they want. Patrick's been focusing on listening to what the man needs, not what Patrick wants to sell him—resulting in the customer trading his valuable money for a more valuable table saw.

Jackie made a mental note. Did Jim realize that their conversation was already addressing some of her cares?

"When things happen as we want them to, an effective conversation has to take place. Think about the latte you got this morning at the Coffee Shack."

Jackie was surprised he'd even noticed.

"You went to the Coffee Shack and ordered a latte, the barista then made the latte, and you exchanged money for the latte."

"An effective conversation and we both got our needs addressed," Jackie nodded.

"Why are you and I talking right now?" Jim asked.

"Because you and I had a conversation." The puzzle pieces started falling into place.

"An organization is simply a network of conversations. The more the conversations are effective, the more the organization coordinates action and gets what it sets out to get."

"I'm guessing that's not exactly the case with ineffective conversations."

"Let's continue the walkabout, find one and see." Jim

headed off, almost as if he'd anticipated Jackie's observation before she'd even made it. As they walked toward the warehouse, Jim pointed out examples of effective conversations, things like products on shelves where they should be and clean floors.

"All the results of effective conversations," Jackie noted.

As they entered the warehouse, Jim walked Jackie directly to the table laden with stacks of unfinished and messy invoices where Jackie and Cynthia had spoken earlier.

"What do you make of this?" Jim asked, indicating the disorder.

"A big pile of ineffective conversations," Jackie smirked.

"Why do you say that?"

"Invoices that are in various states of organization and completion, but in reality no one knows for sure, because nobody's talking effectively about them."

"Explain."

"A lot of those invoices come from the retail store, and the sales people put them here because nobody's ever talked about where they should go. Cynthia and her staff haven't had effective conversations about how to deal with this because they are totally focused on getting product shipped. I am even seeing the accounting and IT departments pitching in because they're not having effective conversations with the warehouse or the store about what to do with all the paperwork. It's a big mess, and nobody's getting their needs met." Jackie's brow furrowed.

"Anything else?" Jim asked.

Jackie's answer didn't come easily. "I see that non-existent conversations between Mark and me created this, too." Jackie looked to Jim. "Which is what you mean by missing conversations." The realization sapped her energy and forced her to face the reality she'd been working so hard to ignore. "In addition to getting everyone else to start communicating, Mark and I need to have some difficult conversations that aren't happening—frankly, a problem he and I started having as teenagers after Mom passed away. He may not even be aware that they're needed."

"If you're open to it," Jim replied softly, "I think that is a conversation we can explore in due time. But first there's one more thing I'd like you to observe. You've shared quite a range of emotions in our conversations today," Jim said, completely without judgment.

"I have. I'm sorry."

"Don't apologize; humans are emotional beings. In fact, I want to challenge you to observe the organization from an emotional standpoint also."

Jackie regarded him, not completely following.

"When you were excited about what we were learning from observing Patrick, what was your mood or emotion?"

"Excited. Optimistic."

"What about when you talked about Mark just now?"

Jackie let loose an inadvertent sigh. "Sad and pessimistic."

"What seems possible when you're feeling gloomy rather than hopeful and upbeat?"

"A lot less. When we watched Patrick I felt like anything was possible for this company and for me. Even thinking about the Mark situation makes me want to just go away and hide."

"Which is why I want you to explore the overall mood and emotion of the organization. Remember, when I said that the organizational culture you have is one-hundred percent perfect to get the results you are getting?"

Jackie nodded.

"That's because moods and emotions are a predisposition to action. If we have an organization that's mired in resignation, resentment, anger, and frustration what will be possible in that culture?"

"Not much," replied Jackie.

"I agree. So here's your homework from now until we meet again for burritos in two weeks. Observe this organization from the perspective of whether or not effective, ineffective, or missing conversations are going on—and secondly, what moods and emotions you see and where you see them."

The thought of what she might find only darkened Jackie's mood. But then she realized in order to fix things, she was going to have to step up and become a true leader, and sooner than she expected. As she considered this, she was surprised to find an emotion filling her. Ambition.

New Eyes

The next few days were a whirlwind for Jackie as she endeavored to see the world—and Perfectly Square—through new eyes. Immediately after her conversation with Jim, she embarked on a walkabout of her own. She started by heading to the back corner of the warehouse where she suspected, as is the case with many warehouses, the fruits of ineffective conversations end up. Sure enough, she discovered a pile of old chairs, broken pallets, trash, and boxes of "stuff," all of which had been there so long they were covered in a dense blanket of dust—relics of ineffective and missing conversations. In an ineffective conversation, someone could have told a member of the warehouse team to "get rid of the old chairs," and for lack of clear direction, that person figured this corner was as good as any place to "get rid of the old chairs." Its ongoing existence could be the product of missing conversations because it showed Jackie that no one—possibly from her father before he died to Mark, to Cynthia, and even herself—had come back to this location and had a conversation about cleaning it up. She saw how the clutter was a metaphor for Perfectly Square's dysfunctional aspects of its culture. Where else were there "dirty corners" in the organization?

Jackie worked her way back toward the store. Along the way she saw Patrick helping in the warehouse again, talking with Jamie Sanders. She stopped behind some storage racks before they saw her.

"Come on, man, it's not that bad. I really have fun when I come back here and work in the warehouse." Patrick sounded enthusiastic.

"I agree, but at times it becomes overwhelming," Jamie replied dejectedly. "I try to keep positive and think most of the time I am; it's just that it seems like there is never an end to the chaos, we never seem to get ahead of the game. I have a bad day here and then I go home and can't relax there because I'm thinking about work, and then the next day it starts all over again. My family thinks I'm turning into a real jerk."

From her vantage point, Jackie felt a little guilty for eavesdropping. But only a little—she was more interested in gaining some valuable, and candid, insights.

"Doesn't Cynthia help?" asked Patrick.

"She tries, but she's more overwhelmed than I am. It's a wonder she doesn't quit."

At that moment, Cynthia entered. "Who's over-whelmed and who's quitting?" she asked, pretty sure that she was the subject of conversation.

Jamie's only answer was the sudden flush of red in his cheeks.

"I may get down at times, but I believe this is a great place to work and it hasn't whipped me yet; I still have some fight left in me," Cynthia said with a disarming smile. "Now get back to work or I will do what it takes to make you both want to quit!"

The others never knew Jackie was there, but in this brief conversation she observed many moods and emotions. She saw Patrick's optimism offset by Jamie's pessimism and dejection. She empathized with Jamie and believed he wasn't a bad person; he was just overwhelmed. Coming to work day after day to a situation that seems like you will never get ahead would wear anyone down. The warehouse was doing many things well; fortunately, just a small percentage of orders weren't getting shipped. That indicated a mix of effective and ineffective conversations. She saw how Cynthia was—for the most part—optimistic, but like anyone had bad days. As Jackie mulled things over, it occurred to her that a big missing conversation was a strategic one about how they wanted to perform and be as an organization. Things she would have to bring up with Jim, she thought with an involuntary tightening of her stomach. As unpleasant as the prospect of opening up the hornet's nest of issues with Jim was, she knew she couldn't wait two weeks to explore this deeper.

As she concluded her walkabout, Jackie experienced some more troubling conversations in the store with Jason Shumway. She sensed he was not telling her everything and was trying to control the subject and length of their conversations. In short, when they talked it was if he was hiding things. Jackie noted that Jason seemed to be having conversations with others about fellow employees and the leadership of the store. If she had to put a name to the emotion he exuded when they spoke it would be arrogance—as if Jackie, his superior, was meddling in his business. Jackie knew that there needed to be some serious conversations with Jason. She was also aware that the conversations might create powerful emotions for Jason; certainly he was creating strong emotions for her—and they weren't good.

Jackie continued to see moods and emotions and various forms of conversations (and non-conversations) wherever she went. She applied Jim's principles to her observations and realized how accurate and elegant they truly were: a happy customer meant an effective conversation had taken place. An unhappy customer meant an ineffective conversation had transpired on some level. Confusion, inefficiency, and redundancy meant ineffective or missing conversations. She started to see a correlation between effective conversations and more positive moods, as well as a connection between ineffective and missing conversations and negative emotions and apathy. Jim was right. The culture that Perfectly Square had was 100 percent perfect to get the results they were getting. If someone wanted to change the results, he or she would have to change the conversations that they, as an organization, were having. That person would also have to change the mood of the organization. They were all related, and they all seemed to show up in this thing called culture. Did Mark have what it took to be the person to make those changes? To create the new culture that Perfectly Square so obviously needed? Jackie didn't want to consider the answers, at least not then and there.

Her next conversation with Jim was going to be an interesting one.

The Second Burrito

As much as Jackie couldn't wait to share with Jim all she was seeing, she was so busy that she decided it would be best to hold her thoughts until their Wednesday conversation over coffee and burritos. She continued to observe and carefully note the conversations and the moods of the organization.

This time when she walked through the Coffee Shack's door at 8 a.m. sharp, Jim was waiting for her with two juicy burritos, a black coffee and a fresh, steaming latte. After exchanging pleasantries, they got down to business.

"So, what did you notice?" Jim asked, with an air of excited anticipation.

"Where to start?" Sipping her latte, Jackie tried to resist the urge to overwhelm Jim with all she had to share. "Let me just say I see what you mean that everything is a conversation. It was very helpful just to stand back and observe. I found I could tie nearly everything at the company, good and bad, to the conversation that led to it. I saw a few effective conversations, more ineffective conversations, and a ton of missing conversations." She toyed with her burrito for a moment. "Many of them center around my relationship with Mark as a co-owner of the company. I'm seeing that he and I have lots to talk about if the business is going to survive, let alone thrive. And that all three types of conversations have created our culture at Perfectly Square."

"What about moods and emotions?" Jim asked, taking a bite.

"They were everywhere, a mixture of both positive and negative. When they were positive, I felt positive, and when they were negative I could feel myself being drawn down. It's as if the moods and emotions were conversations themselves."

"Great observation, Jackie. In many respects, moods and emotions are conversations. Let me show you what I mean." Jim set down his fork. "I'm going to ask you a question. The first time you answer, I want you to say the words, 'I will.' But I want you to say them from the mood of resignation and resentment, as if you are only saying them because you have no other choice."

Jackie nodded.

"Okay, here's the question. Jackie, will you show up for the team meeting tomorrow and lead the conversation about the new computer changes?"

"I will," Jackie replied in such a resentful and resigned manner that it seemed she was a prisoner.

"Great. Now try it again, but this time, answer, 'I will' with as much ambition and excitement as you can muster. Jackie, will you show up for the team meeting tomorrow and lead the conversation about the new computer changes?"

"I WILL!" exclaimed Jackie, almost jumping out of her seat with enthusiasm and excitement. She took a moment to assess what had happened. "Wow, Jim. What an amazing difference. I wasn't just *saying* 'I will'; I was *feeling* it."

"Remember this: moods and emotions are a predisposition to action. The emotion in which you answered me told me what was possible. If you were a participant in the first scenario, how motivated do you think you would be to get on board with the new computer changes?"

"Not at all."

"Me either. How about the second scenario?"

"Very motivated. Even if I didn't really believe in the changes, if that's how the leader showed up I'm sure I'd get on board."

"You and everybody else. That's why I wanted you to explore the organizational culture from the perspectives of conversations and moods and emotions. It's where these two concepts overlap that determine what is possible in the culture."

"You know, it was interesting, the more that positive emotions and conversations occurred, the energy of the room or the team seemed to flow better—the situation became more alive."

"It is funny you should say the word 'flow,' Jackie, because that's something we will talk about in our future conversations. Flow is at the root of what we are exploring. For right now, what questions did this exploration lead you to?"

"To what's next and how do I change this culture."

"And we're going to get to that. But for now, let's enjoy these burritos."

Jackie couldn't help but notice how much better hers tasted after spending just a few minutes with Jim.

Visioning the Future

When I took over my battalion, my boss, a super effective leader, shared with me another of his leadership tenets, which works in any organization, not just the military. And as I said before, I call it LeadershipFlow." Jim took a moment to savor the warm coffee, then pulled out the napkin with the diagram he had drawn at their last meeting. This time he added the words, "Visioning the Future" to the upper left section.

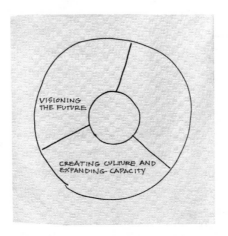

"He told me this: one of the two most critical things a leader does is create a vision of the future that others want to be a part of."

Jackie listened intently, what was left of her breakfast now forgotten.

"Let's break that down. What do companies spend billions of dollars on to get you to buy their products?"

Jackie didn't have to think long. "Advertising."

"That's right. Their goal is to make their car or gadget so appealing that you'll go out and spend your hard-earned money to own it. And they're more than willing to invest an enormous amount of their assets to make this happen. Leadership and creating a vision of a company are no different. Your goal is to create a vision of the company so clear to your team members that they see themselves as part of that vision, and will spend their talents and energies to make that vision come alive."

Jackie was with him every step of the way. "The main reason I came back home was the future I could see and wanted to help create for Perfectly Square. To build on what my parents started and make this place thrive not just for me and my family, but for the families of people like Cynthia and Patrick, too. It may sound a bit corny, but I also want to allow woodworkers like you to build their passions, one cut at a time," Jackie laughed. "Maybe there is a company vision statement somewhere in there."

"You may be more right than you think," Jim smiled. "That's the power of a vision; it brings energies and people alive. Remember earlier when I pointed out that you used the word 'flow'?"

"I've been counting the minutes until we could circle back."

"There's a researcher by the name of Mihaly Csikszentmihalyi—please don't ask me to spell it—who in the sixties and seventies studied happiness. He conducted a scientific, worldwide study of what made people happy. After interviewing people from all cultures, all backgrounds, all walks of life, he found a common answer.

Those who were truly happy shared that they were doing something they loved; an athlete, a homemaker, a rice farmer, a doctor, it didn't really matter. They all loved how they spent their days, and talked about this state of being where everything kind of 'flowed.' Csikszentmihalyi recognized this 'flow' state was really what it meant to be our best as humans. You're a runner, right?"

Jackie nodded. "I love it. I'm a different person when I'm running. I forget about what I'm doing, I'm lost in my thoughts, and totally in the zone. Sometimes I forget that I'm running and go longer than I planned." She smiled at Jim. "Flow."

"We've all experienced Flow at times. We lose track of time, our concentration increases, our creativity goes through the roof, we become the bike, the tool, whatever it is, we come alive as humans. For me it's when I am doing woodworking; it's like I can feel the wood and how to cut it. Time doesn't stand still—it ceases to exist. I'm perfectly in the moment, doing what I do best. This is the power of Flow. To be at our best, doing our best."

"I've found it when I'm totally absorbed in a project or reading a good book or talking to a close friend." Jackie took a moment to remember the feeling. "Not only do I feel more alive as it's happening, it spreads to other things throughout my day."

"It's physiological. When a person's experiencing Flow, the body produces powerful neurochemicals such as dopamine, norepinephrine, and endorphins. When we are in Flow we are getting high, but through our natural way the body produces great feelings. Most of the common street drugs somehow mimic or affect the natural neurochemicals that our bodies produce. But I think there's more to it. There's an enormous power to being fully involved in the moment; that's where magic happens."

Jackie took a moment to absorb this truth. "To be in Flow is to be at our best."

"Now, let's take Flow and tie it to leadership. Most common definitions of leadership talk in some form about getting results." Jackie could tell from Jim's expression that he disagreed. "To me, leadership is about how you tap into the flow of the people who are on your team. If you as a leader tap the Flow state of your followers, they will be at their best; they will be in powerful, positive moods. Without even consciously realizing it, they'll be having fun and will bring all of that energy to the task at hand. Getting results is not the goal of leadership; results are the by-product of finding Flow and bringing out the best in your team."

"Find and tap Flow, and the results will follow," Jackie nodded.

"That's why the vision of a company is so important. Everyone has to see his or her future in the vision. The more they do, the more they see that they can be their best, the more they can tap Flow—and the greater the company and everyone involved with it becomes."

"We have to come up with a powerful vision that's not about sales and numbers, but about moods and emotions and bringing people alive. The clearer it is and the more we have conversations around it, the more we can start to bridge the gap of what we currently have."

"No wonder your old man was always bragging about

how smart you are," Jim smiled warmly. "We start with the culture we have, which is one-hundred percent perfect in getting the results we are currently getting. To change that, we need to get clear on the behaviors, moods, and emotions we want to see, and then we must have effective conversations to get from where we are to where we want to be. Sounds simple, but it can be difficult to achieve."

Jim gave Jackie a long, hard look. "So I'll just come out and ask you, Jackie. What's the vision of Perfectly Square? What are the behaviors, moods, and emotions you want to be working toward?"

"I was feeling great until you asked that question," Jackie said, but in a mood of ambition, not resignation. "I feel like this is my homework until our next talk."

Jim's face crinkled with a reassuring grin. "Can't wait to hear how it goes."

Looking for a Vision

"Jackie's mixed emotions roiled within her as she arrived for work after breakfast with Jim. On the one hand, she was excited because through her conversations with Jim, she felt she was really gaining clarity on what the organization needed to focus on to have a prosperous future. On the other hand, just thinking about the uncertainty of what the future would look like for Perfectly Square tugged on the ever-tightening knot in her stomach. Where did she fit in? Was Mark the leader for the future? Could they chart a path for growth and build a high performing organization? Her attempts to silence the voices of doubt and worry only made them louder.

She'd planned to spend the morning with Jason Shumway getting more insight into the day-to-day operations of the store; she had the afternoon booked with Mark. It would be a busy day with ample opportunities to explore the vision of the future that leaders were working toward—and hopefully be constructive, not destructive.

Her time with Jason was uneventful, going over the latest store schedules and logistics of a big annual four-day weekend sales event. Jason was knowledgeable about the running of the store, having been an employee for twenty-plus years. He also seemed to really know woodworking, which gave him a deep understanding of their products and he appeared to have a solid grasp of the business side of things. Still, Jackie noted tension between them, unsure if it was he not trusting her, just the way he was, or something else. Little did she realize that a major clue was about to walk in the door.

As they were finishing, a customer arrived and asked for Jason. After exchanging pleasantries, the customer gave Jason a knowing smile. It seemed strange, Jackie noted, for a man to whom he'd just been introduced.

"I'm looking to buy some tools and I've heard you're the man to talk to about a deal."

Though Jason tried to cover, Jackie couldn't ignore the way he uncomfortably cleared his throat.

"We don't make deals below our already low prices," Jason replied matter-of-factly. Then, with a hint of salesman's charm added, "but we do have our big sale coming up and we'll be offering some markdowns then."

Jackie noticed that the customer seemed confused, as if he'd gotten some erroneous information. When he persisted on asking for a discount, Jason snapped and told him in no uncertain terms that Perfectly Square did not operate that way. The way the customer turned and abruptly walked out the door, creating a bit of a stir for the employees and other customers, did not escape Jackie, nor did it sit particularly well with her.

First, Jason appeared to be rude to a customer, pushing a potential sale out the door. But there was more. The way the customer had referred to Jason as, 'the man to talk to for deals' had a dark undercurrent. In a visceral way, it seemed to Jackie that something was not completely honest about Jason Shumway. Jackie immediately thought back to her conversation with Jim. At the very least, an ineffective conversation between Jason and a customer had just occurred ... which meant there was a missing conversation with Jason that she needed to make happen.

As she considered which conversation to address first, Jason beat her to the punch. "Yeah, we get guys like that in the store every once in a while wanting some kind of special discount. I have no idea why they think I'm the guy to talk to, but we already have great prices and cutting them any further really messes up our margins." He gave what seemed to Jackie like an affected shrug. "Oh well, maybe some neighbor told him about our great prices and he got the wrong idea." He flashed Jackie a 'just between you and me' smile. "Guys like that are a pain in the butt," he said like they were best friends. "I don't have the time to waste with them."

Jackie considered her response carefully. She knew she should explore what had just happened, but the prospect of confronting Jason—at least then and there—didn't feel right. So she opted for a nod and, "I bet. Some customers can be a pain," almost as if she agreed with him. The moment the words were out of her mouth she regretted them, unable to shake the feeling that she was somehow letting Jason off the hook. She rationalized the missing conversation by telling herself she would talk to him when the time was right, but ultimately she let herself and the company down and she knew it. She vowed she would not make the same mistake again.

Jackie spent the rest of the morning talking to employees to see what they thought the vision of the company was. The conversations she had were both enlightening and disheartening. It became obvious that there was not a clear idea of Perfectly Square's organizational identity.

She witnessed several examples that ran counter to what the company should be aspiring to: the unsettling conversation with Jason, the dirty corners of the warehouse, negative talk and emotions at every level of the organization. Balancing this were several bright spots that gave her cause for optimism. She saw customers who really loved to come to the store and talk about woodworking with the knowledgeable sales staff. She saw that the company's ability to help woodworkers complete projects one step at a time had created a real niche. Team members like Cynthia and Patrick were clearly committed to making things better. She was also quite aware of where there seemed to be Flow and where it was stagnant.

She was glad she had time on the calendar with Mark that afternoon because it was becoming abundantly clear there needed to be new conversations, and those conversations needed to focus on what she and Mark wanted to create as the owners of the company. If they didn't have these conversations, she feared that Perfectly Square would no longer be a rudderless ship, but one with so many holes in it that it would sink. She hoped Mark would open up to her the way he used to, and that she would find the confidence and insight she needed to mend those holes in time.

Mark Andrews

Mark grew up in a world that many would envy. His parents loved him and Jackie and were very involved their lives—until his mother passed away—while working hard to create a family-owned business that provided them with a very comfortable life. Mark and Jackie attended the best schools and never really wanted for anything—except in Mark's case, to be his own person. He was born with an innate aptitude and affinity for painting, and through hard work and natural ability had become quite good at it. His mother, while alive, was his biggest fan; his father, wanting what he thought was best for his son, allowed Mark to pursue his love of art but always believed that Mark needed to have a "real" career to build his future on, not the mercurial, unstable life of a professional artist. From Fred's perspective, that meant Mark following in Fred's footsteps and eventually running Perfectly Square. Not soliciting his son's feelings on this provided a perfect example of a missing conversation.

Mark began working at Perfectly Square when he was quite young, though he found woodworking to be too mechanical and not creative enough. During high school, Mark worked primarily in the warehouse and did a variety of odd jobs for his dad. When the time came for college, Fred wanted Mark to attend the University of New Mexico, continue working at the store, and eventually get a business degree, quietly put his artistic journey to rest. In a rare show of independence, Mark went against his father's wishes and decided to attend Arizona State in Phoenix. This choice represented a sort of compromise as ASU had a great art program and Perfectly Square had a store in Phoenix close to the campus, enabling Mark to still work for the company in his spare time. From Fred's perspective, this also added a layer of growth for Mark as it gave him the opportunity see how they did things in one of the other stores.

Much to his dad's chagrin, when Mark graduated from college he took a year off and spent time in Europe—mainly in France, especially Paris—further immersing himself in art while working part time as a barista in a Left Bank café. It proved to be one of the best years of Mark's life; however, the strain of repeatedly having to answer to his dad eventually wore him down, and one day he carefully folded his dreams, packed them away, and dragged himself home to start his 'career' in Perfectly Square's Albuquerque store. He worked without complaint and a fair amount of initiative as the Store Manager and over time he became more deeply enmeshed in the business. His 'marriage' to the business became official with his dad's heart attack. Whether or not he was ready for it, Mark became CEO and part owner of Perfectly Square with his sister, though this was a challenge as Jackie was overseas in the Air Force.

Mark never dared share with anyone that he was miserable. He did the job out of a combination of guilt and his heartfelt desire to be a good son and brother, but despite his best efforts, he could never fully conceal these deeply buried feelings of resentment and resignation from those around him. They showed up in his lack of presence as a leader. Rather than engaging and imparting his vision for the future (if he had one), Mark instead spent his days in the comfortable seclusion of his office, caught up in minutiae and ultimately unimportant data, a shield against having to step up and take action as a leader.

Jackie knew of Mark's ambivalence better than anyone. As Mark and his father wrestled over the competing visions of Mark's future, Jackie had been a spectator to the battles, and dealt with it by jumping into her own activities. She truly wanted what was best for her brother, and even though she fully understood her father's wishes, always felt that Mark should chart his own, authentic path. When Mark stepped in to run the company, Jackie hoped their relationship would improve; however, the further he got in, the more distant he became, hoping to shield her from his unhappiness and create the impression of being fulfilled with his lot and life. And so Jackie played along, still believing that with every fiber of his being Mark did not want to be CEO.

A Conversation with Mark

After lunch and time to rehearse and refine her approach, Jackie took a deep breath and strode into Mark's office, located between the warehouse and the show room. She wanted to exude warmth and confidence, and yet couldn't imagine how she would even begin to have the missing conversation that had been needed for so long.

"How are you?" she smiled as she entered. At least the first three words came easily.

"Hey, Ace!" Mark replied, using his nickname for Jackie since they were kids. It came from their father's way of using "aces" as his way to describe something that was the best. And that was how Mark regarded his sister: as the best.

Despite his sincere attempt to appear upbeat, as always, Jackie could see the unhappiness and restlessness in his eyes. "Ready to chat?" she asked, not completely sure she was herself.

"Sure," said Mark, crossing behind her to close the door before returning to his desk. "So, what have you discovered on your travels?"

She shared with him the ideas of effective, ineffective, and missing conversations and how they determine what is possible. She shared her experiences of the 'dirty corners' in the warehouse, the many conversations she witnessed, and Jim's thoughts on moods and emotions and how they are a predisposition to action. She found herself getting truly excited as she told him about Flow and the concept of Visioning the Future. Eventually she found herself running out of things to talk about, other than the elephant in the room. She chose her words carefully, deliberately. "All of this discovery has pointed me toward what I see as a huge missing conversation, one I think you and I as the owners of this company need to have."

"And what is that?" Mark replied tensely.

For Jackie, this was the moment of truth. She hoped he would understand that her words were coming from her love for him and seeing him struggle for years to find himself and become the person he wanted to be. "I think we have a huge issue, which is—I don't think you really want to work at Perfectly Square, let alone be the CEO. I think you took the CEO role out of a feeling of responsibility to Dad's memory and the family, but really, you know it, Mom knew it, your girlfriend Emma knows it, anyone who knows you knows it: you are an artist and you want to be an artist. Your heart's just not in this job—and it shows."

For a moment, Mark betrayed no reaction and in that instant, Jackie imagined he was relieved to have someone finally articulate what he'd been holding inside for so long, that finally he could relax, breathe, and be who he really is instead of pretending to be somebody or something else. Instead, his words were a punch to her solar plexus.

"And what the hell would you know about it?" he barked, his face flushing, his voice quivering with emotion. "Where were you when the family needed help, when somebody had to set aside their grief and step into this role and get the job done? You were off saving the world, while I was trying to save the company. Who are you to come swooping in at the eleventh hour and tell me my heart's not in it?" Mark rose from his chair, and if Jackie didn't know him better she would've feared that he would physically strike her.

"I've poured myself into this company, I've done what nobody else is willing to do and I've done a damn good job of it! Do you see us hemorrhaging money? Do you see people losing their jobs? Do you see me taking what Mom and Dad spent their lives building and running it into the ground? Could I do things better; hell, yes. But I have kept this company going when nobody else could be bothered! Did I set aside my dreams to do the right thing? You're damn straight I did, and if you want to come in here and have a missing conversation, how about thanking me for what I've done?"

Jackie had never seen her brother like this before, certainly not with her. "Mark, I only—"

"You said what you had to say." He sat down and began furiously rifling through the papers on his desk. "Now do us both a favor and get the hell out. I've got work to do."

And from that second on, it was if Jackie was no longer in the room.

Not sure what else to do, Jackie calmly gathered her things and walked out the door wondering if she had not only failed to save the company, but had destroyed her relationship with her brother in the process.

The Third Burrito

Jackie stepped into The Coffee Shack twenty minutes before her next meeting with Jim, a product of not wanting him to buy her breakfast again—and even more, the fact that she'd been lying awake since 3:41 a.m. (she'd checked) wracked with concern and regret over her conversation with Mark. After finding a quiet spot, she paid the waitress in advance and told her to bring out Jim's coffee and the two burritos right at 8 a.m. She got her latte and tried to figure out how things could've gone so terribly wrong.

Jim walked in precisely at eight, just as his coffee and burrito were arriving. "You're good, but next time it's on me," smiled Jim.

"Oh, this." Jackie made the best attempt to be playful that she could muster. "I don't know how they knew you'd be here at 8 a.m. sharp and want a burrito and black coffee, but since it's here, enjoy, my compliments."

Unfortunately for Jackie, Jim was every bit the student of human nature that she was. "So you want to tell me what's wrong?" he asked, biting into his burrito.

"I had the missing conversation with Mark."

"That's good," Jim replied.

"Not exactly. In fact, it couldn't have gone worse. Up until my mom died, he and I never argued. About anything. Somehow we were always in sync, almost could read each other the way they say twins can. After Mom died, things changed. And since Dad died, there's been many missing conversations, personal and professional."

Jim considered his answer while he stirred his coffee. "Sometimes there's a reason conversations go missing for long periods of time. But just because they can be difficult is no excuse not to have them."

"Even if it means crushing your brother's feelings?"

"Sometimes pain is a sign that you're growing. I wouldn't jump to any conclusions too quickly. You're a good person; Mark is, too. He knows better than anyone how much you care for him, and that you only want what's best."

"I doubt he's thinking that right now."

"You never know. Give him some time. And don't beat yourself up for doing what needed to be done. Being a leader doesn't always mean being popular. So, setting Mark aside, what else did you observe?"

"I've got so much to share. I have still been seeing many examples of all three kinds of conversations. Many of the missing ones, like the one I had with Mark, have to do with the vision of the company and what we want to create. We really don't have a vision of where we want to go, of what we want to be as an organization when we grow up." She elaborated on what she had seen about the lack of vision and how it was creating the issues in the warehouse. Together, they explored how the lack of vision was affecting other departments and was leading to frustration and infighting. Soon enough, the chat drifted back to Jackie's conversation with Mark.

"It became more and more obvious to me that our leaders aren't sharing a vision because they don't have clarity on what it might be and the two people who should have the vision, Mark and me, haven't been leading."

"And when you said so, that's when the train went off the tracks."

"I want Mark to succeed as the CEO, but I know that he doesn't want to be the leader of the company. And his anger and defensiveness may hurt—but they don't change my opinion one bit."

Jim took this in. "Remember how I said that a leader did two critical things, the first being Visioning the Future that others aspire to? Well, now it's time to explore the second part of that statement."

Cultivating Other Leaders
and Teams

"To create high-performing organizations we need to have clarity about the conversations, moods, and emotions we want to create," Jim started. "We have to be able to know the behaviors we want from our organization, because that's tied to creating Flow—and then we can start to create the vision.

"And how do we do that?" Jackie asked, feeling overwhelmed at the magnitude of the task that lay ahead.

"We need leaders and teams that are committed to that vision," continued Jim. "So the second thing a leader has to do is to create other leaders and teams that are aligned and committed to the vision." From his binder, Jim removed the napkin he shared in their last conversation. This time in the lower right section he wrote the words, "Cultivating other Leaders and Teams."

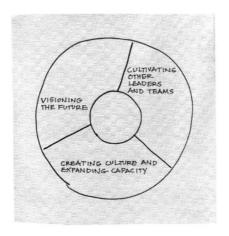

"Sounds simple," interjected Jackie. "But at the risk of repeating myself, how?"

"By having effective conversations about things like moods and emotions, we determine what it is that people care about, what it would take for them to be committed to the vision. If you think about it, it's no different than the culture we currently have, which is a result of the conversations we are having."

"And not having," added Jackie.

"Exactly. That, plus the moods and emotions people show up with determine what is possible. To change the culture, leaders must have the necessary conversations effectively in order to create Flow on a daily basis. The role of the leader is to shape more leaders aligned to the vision."

"Mark and I aren't clear on what we want from the organization, so how can anyone else be?" Jackie sipped her latte, her mind racing. "I need to explore how to create effective leaders and teams so that we can continue to build this organization into what it should be."

"A good place to start is to look for what I call your studs and duds, to use some military lingo. Many times people try to focus on the entire organization. The challenge is, and research proves this, that most people are followers and not leaders. Your job is to find the leaders who are aligned with the vision, who have a higher proportional influence with others, reward them, and get them to join your cause. These are the studs. But you need to find your duds, too."

Jackie immediately thought of Jason Shumway.

"These are the people who have a higher proportional influence with others," Jim continued, "but they resist vision and change, and in some cases even fight them. Conversations need to address their behaviors and their effects on others minimized."

"Does that mean all the duds need to be fired?" The idea of confronting more people on the heels of her blowup with Mark was daunting.

"Not necessarily. Often, they see change as a danger for them or their team. And because they have influence, they can sway others' thinking."

"Because many people are followers, not leaders. I'm wondering if it's always going to be obvious who the studs and duds are. For example, Cynthia. I would have sworn she was a dud when I first met her, but I couldn't have been more wrong."

"It can be tricky, which is why it's critical for leaders to engage in effective conversations and explore to see who is buying into the vision."

"That is, when we have a vision," joked Jackie, her mood marginally improving. Then as quickly as it buoyed, it sank again. "Which brings me back to Mark. What if he doesn't really want to lead or buy in or contribute to the conversation? What if he makes it clear that I'm not welcome at Perfectly Square anymore?"

"I highly doubt that's going to happen," Jim said gently. "Remember, we're not assessing whether or not someone is a good or bad person, simply if he or she is helping to create and bring the vision alive or not. Sometimes it's the senior leaders who most need to go and get out of the way. Looks like more conversations need to be had."

He could see the worry etched on her face.

"You don't have to solve it all right now. Look at it this way. If you could only have one conversation with one person you think is critical to the success of the company, who would that person be? And if you could only have one conversation with the person you think you need to address buying or not buying in, who would that be?"

Jackie nodded, already knowing who this would be.

"I haven't even shared with you the most critical and difficult LeadershipFlow tenet there is, but never fear, that's for a future conversation."

"Good, I'm feeling like my plate is plenty full right now," Jackie sighed. "Overflowing, in fact."

"We'll chat again once you've had some time to find other leaders and teams that you think will help take this company to the next level," Jim replied.

"As well as those who won't," Jackie replied in a tone of fortitude mixed with sorrow.

As they said their goodbyes on the sidewalk in front of The Coffee Shack, Jackie felt a ray of sunshine among the clouds. The light grew stronger when Jim added, "You did the right thing with Mark. Give it some time."

For the first time in twenty-four hours, the knot in Jackie's stomach ever so slightly loosened.

Starting to Build a Team

For Jackie, running had always been a release, a place where life seemed to find a new perspective—Flow. She'd been running a lot since she was back at Perfectly Square. She found that no matter what was happening, a long run seemed to ground every challenge and reset her for the next challenge she faced. Since she had learned about Flow from Jim and she had started to explore what happens in Flow, it all made more sense. It is in Flow that the body's powerful neurochemicals kick in and bring us to our best. That morning's run was especially powerful for Jackie.

It was the day after her third meeting with Jim; she rose early to get a six-miler in before work. As she found her rhythm and her body relaxed, her mind also ran free. Although she was still overwhelmed by all that had happened—as well as what lay before her—she was starting to see a way to navigate the challenges. She had begun to internalize Jim's first two tenets: the culture they had was creating everything that happened, and she was seeing conversations everywhere. On some days it seemed like more were effective than ineffective, but on other days the reverse was true. She was also keenly aware of more and more missing conversations.

She noticed moods and emotions everywhere. There seemed to be days when one team or department was affected by either a positive or negative event, triggering a collective emotion that set the tone for the entire day. She saw positive emotions in employees like Patrick Lee, who seemed to see the world through positive emotions no matter what obstacles or negativity presented themselves. She also saw that Mark's resignation and resentment seemed increasingly to be how he viewed the world, which made her very sad, remembering the bright, optimistic boy she'd grown up with.

Around mile two, Jackie's thinking shifted to the second tenet, Visioning the Future. She thought about her father and what his vision of the company had been. He had been very adamant about certain values that were critical to success for him. Values like honesty, offering a quality product at a fair price, loyalty to the customer, and loyalty to the company. If she was being honest, though, there were qualities he believed in that did not necessarily fit anymore. He believed that employees who were with the company for a long time should be protected, even if they no longer added value, creating a sense of entitlement that was still prevalent in the company. She wrestled with the vision for the future that she and Mark, if they both were going to be a part of the future, would need to create.

The last few miles she started to wrestle with the idea of cultivating other leaders and teams. Who would be the leaders to help take the company into the future? There were bright spots, people like Patrick—positive, hard worker, honest as the day was long and great with customers—the type of person she'd love to clone. There were others who landed more in the middle. She thought about Jim's advice to choose the one person she thought was the most influential in a positive way—as well as the person who was the most influential in a negative way.

The most positive influential leader in the company was Cynthia Hernandez. Cynthia added immeasurable value to the company. She could be a bit overwhelmed at times and when she was, she came across as negative, but Jackie was sure she could have some very positive conversations with her about how to more productively address the issues in the e-commerce/warehouse department. As for the negative influencer, that would be Jason Shumway. Jason concerned Jackie for many reasons. He was the leader of the aforementioned Table Saw Mafia—the remnants of the company from earlier days—who still had that sense of entitlement she needed to address. There was also the issue of his trustworthiness and honesty.

She decided she'd start her conversations with Cynthia and Jason. And, of course, the third person she also knew she would need to continue her conversations with. It was in this frame of mind that she rounded the corner onto the block where she'd rented a house—and at first didn't notice the familiar man sitting on her front steps.

She slowed as Mark stood to greet her.

"Hey."

"Hey. I figured when you weren't home that you must be out on one of your runs. I was hoping to catch you before you left."

Sister and brother studied each other's faces for a hint of what the other might be feeling.

"I'm sorry I missed you," Jackie finally replied. "It would've been nice." The fact that he was here and wasn't yelling at her had to be positive, right?

"Got another mile or two in you? It's cool if we walk."

"Yeah, sure," said Jackie, thrilled at the open door. "Which way?"

Mark looked up and down the street. "I don't know. How about thataway?" he pointed.

"Perfect," Jackie smiled.

The morning air was cool and refreshing as they walked. Jackie remembered that soon it would be warm even at this early hour.

"I've been thinking a lot about our conversation," Mark ventured as they made their way down the sidewalk toward a small neighborhood park.

"You and me both."

"You really hit me hard. It hurt."

"I know and I'm sorry. You may never believe it, but I did it out of love for you, for what I thought was best for everyone."

"I haven't slept much since then," Mark said, "which gave me a lot of time to paint." He couldn't help but smile. "It's always been my escape, my therapy. Like running is for you. I started working last night about ten and just put the brush down a little while ago. I couldn't believe six hours had gone by. It felt like fifteen minutes." Mark took a long pause as he stopped by a fence protecting the park's small playground. "It got me thinking about what you were saying about Flow. When I paint, I'm totally in it … couldn't stop it from happening if I wanted it to." He took a moment before choosing his next words. When he did, he looked Jackie directly in the eye. "Something I've never felt at work. Not once, not ever. It was very difficult hearing what you had to say—all the more so because it was something I've never had the courage to admit to myself. But you were right. I don't want to be CEO. I'm doing a poor job of it and it shows."

"Mark, you're—"

"It's okay. You were right," Mark said with a combination of relief and surprise at how good it felt to finally say it. "It's always been a struggle for me." They continued walking. "I've always wanted to be an artist, even if it meant never having two cents to rub together, but after Dad … well, I just felt like it was my job to run the business. No offense, Jackie, but Dad always felt like it was my job to follow in his footsteps."

"I know that, and he made a good choice. The problem is, it was his dream, not yours."

Mark nodded. "Still, I'm not sure I'm ready to step aside. Part of me feels like I'd be letting Dad down. Letting myself down. I hate the idea of walking away before the job is done."

"I get that. The thing is," Jackie continued, "no matter how hard you try to 'like' your job, it will never be what you really want and you'll only be miserable for the rest of your career." Her words were difficult for Mark to hear, but he recognized them as the truth. "We need to keep having conversations about the vision and direction of this company."

"I'd like that," Mark said.

As they continued to talk, Jackie realized that as difficult as the conversation was, and that more uncomfortable talks most certainly awaited them, it was opening a future for the business and bringing Flow alive in her. By the time they talked about Jason, Mark was overwhelmed with deep emotions. His past with his father and his feelings of responsibility still clutched at him, yet for the first time he could remember, he felt the stirrings of ambition and freedom.

By the time they returned to Jackie's house, they both felt relieved, refreshed, and revitalized. "I know a great place for burritos and coffee, if you're interested," Jackie offered.

"The Coffee Shack? You took the words right out of my mouth."

"Give me twenty minutes to shower, and then we'll head over." Jackie turned to go inside when Mark stopped her with a gentle touch to her arm.

"I know it couldn't have been easy for you to come see me and have the conversation we did. But I'm glad you did. Thank you for being honest. It's what I depend on you for."

Jackie blinked back her emotion. "You're welcome."

And then they hugged, warmly and without reservation.

Three Conversations

Even after making in-roads with Mark, and knowing she was on the right path following Jim's advice, Jackie still found herself with a measure of self doubt. No matter how things shook out, Mark was still the CEO of the company and she didn't even really have a title ... yet here she was about to initiate conversations regarding the vision for the company and how to make the company better. Yes, she technically owned one half of the company, but what did she know about running a multi-million dollar business? What would people think as she engaged them in conversation? She was concerned that she was stepping into places where she did not belong. Still, she felt a desire to take action; after all, it was her family's company and there was nothing stopping her from having the conversations. She decided the best place to start was with the easiest one.

After lunch she was back in the warehouse and found Cynthia. "Hey, do you have some free time to chat?"

"For you, of course. My office?" asked Cynthia.

"So what's up?" Cynthia closed her office door and settled behind her desk, filled with work papers and pictures of her kids.

"First, I want to thank you for all you've been doing. You've been fighting an uphill battle since my dad died, not only keeping this place going but really working to make headway into the future."

"Wow, thanks," said Cynthia, relieved. "At times I feel like no one notices all we are doing, only when we seem to drop the ball. Not complaining, but I don't think I've gotten positive feedback for years."

"You deserve it," Jackie said, sincerely. "I really want to talk to you about how we start to address the challenges you and others have been facing and create lasting change that will make our futures secure."

"This is a breath of fresh air! I'm game; it's exciting to actually have conversations about what's possible and not just about where we're failing. We could do so many things to make this place better," Cynthia continued eagerly; "we just need to start working as a team, not a bunch of individuals. Where would you like to start? I have a ton of ideas."

Jackie's conversation with Cynthia lasted nearly two hours, running the gamut from specifics like how they could address the issues with the invoices and shipping to what personnel issues Cynthia thought would help the warehouse. The conversation then shifted to more strategic talk about what they both thought the vision of the company should be and how they could get there. They found themselves effortlessly in Flow as they talked, losing track of time while having a great, and as Jackie would later reflect, effective conversation—what she perceived would be the first of many. If only all her conversations could be so positive and productive.

The next morning Jackie rolled out of bed with a palpable sense of foreboding. As much as she enjoyed the conversation with Cynthia, she dreaded the one with Jason. Even though she'd gone on a long run the day before, she knew she needed another to be at her best when she met with Jason.

She got to the store early to make sure she could find him before things got too busy. She did find him, but as she had seen many times, he was talking to someone in the parking lot—before the store had officially opened. When he saw Jackie, he seemed off balance and quickly terminated the chat.

"Hey, who was that?" Jackie asked as they walked toward the store.

"Oh, just a friend," Jason tried to sound relaxed and off-hand.

Once again, Jackie decided to let it go. She had bigger fish to fry. "I have some things I want to chat with you about; is there a good time today?"

"I'm pretty busy … what's this about?"

"I want to get your thoughts about what we could do to improve and what you think could be the long-term vision of the company."

Jason gave a short laugh as he logged on to the register. "What's to talk about; we sell woodworking equipment. If we just focused on that and quit going off on tangents like the online stuff, we'd be fine."

Jackie found herself having to check her anger at the dismissive way he was treating her. "I want to explore this with you," she said more forcefully. "I thought as a leader of the organization you'd have thoughts and would be open to sharing them."

Jason could see Jackie meant business. "Fine, let's go talk."

He led the way into his office, not waiting for Jackie,

subtly letting her know that she wasn't about to direct where things went. Jackie sat down, noting that Jason's office was more of a shrine, dedicated to Jason and all his golf buddies.

"So. What do you want to talk about?" Jason asked tersely.

"Is something going on? Between us?" Jackie asked, following her gut and surprised at her bluntness.

"Not on my end; everything's great here." Jason's tone clearly embodied the awkwardness in the air.

The conversation continued down hill from that point. The more Jason spoke the more frustrated, angry, and doubtful Jackie became. Jason manipulated the conversation to address his agenda, mentioning everything he saw that was wrong with the company, that there were no issues with his team, but rather with others like Cynthia. "You and your brother need to decide what you are doing, because the company has suffered since your father died," he finally said bluntly, and without apology, looking directly at Jackie as if to say that she and Mark had no place running the company.

Despite her justifiable anger and overpowering desire to fire him on the spot, Jackie knew better than to let her emotions take over. And as much as she hated to admit it, in some sense, she had to agree with him. If she was unblinkingly honest with herself, what did she or Mark really know about running a woodworking supply business?

After twenty-five minutes (that felt like three hours) of hearing Jason's unproductive criticisms and self-serving suggestions, Jackie decided it was time to end the conversation. As much as she wanted to move on, she couldn't deny that there was an element of truth in Jason's diatribe. She spent the rest of the day trying to look busy, but not really accomplishing much. She thought about setting up another meeting with Jim, but knew that she still had to have her next conversation with Mark, and after her conversation with Jason—and initially smoothing things over with her brother—she was not looking forward to it.

In the week and a half that followed, Jackie continued to struggle with the best course of action to take with Jason. The conversation combined with her ongoing observations only made her more suspicious of him and his activities. He always seemed to be looking over his shoulder for her, always having sidebar conversations with people who did not seem to be Perfectly Square's typical customers.

She also kept trying to line up time with Mark to talk. Admittedly, she was not exactly persistent with her attempts and the few times she did check in with him, he was busy reacting to fires, which frankly came as something of a relief. She really wasn't in the mood to continue exploring whether he wanted to be the CEO of the company and perhaps reopen still-healing wounds; and so, to a large degree, she gave into the deep mood of resignation that washed over her. Her sole bright spot was looking ahead to Friday when she and Jim were scheduled to have their next conversation.

Thursday afternoon finally came, and as Jackie drove home from work thinking about what she was going to tell Jim, she reflected that—once again—she'd experienced all three types of conversations: an effective one with Cynthia, an ineffective one with Jason, and a missing one with her brother. She was also keenly aware of her funky mood and how she'd gone from the high emotions of her conversation with Cynthia to the lows after her conversation with Jason.

At least she could share with Jim her awareness of how conversations and moods and emotions create the Perfectly Square's culture. And her occasional desire to just walk away and let somebody else deal with it all.

Friday morning couldn't come quickly enough.

The Fourth Burrito

By now, Jim and Jackie had each accepted that they would take turns buying breakfast. Though Jackie knew full well it was she who was benefiting from Jim's wisdom, she didn't realize Jim was having a blast helping a young leader grow into the great leader she could be. Still, Jackie wasn't surprised to walk in to The Coffee Shack at the appointed time to find Jim with two burritos, a coffee, and a latte waiting for her.

"How go the battles?" asked Jim, giving Jackie a hug.

"I wish I could say better, but it has been a tough few weeks, full of ups and downs," said Jackie, sitting. "I am seeing how much moods and emotions affect the conversations we have and how that determines what we consider to be possible. When I started to look at how to cultivate other leaders and teams, it was quite a mixed bag." She told him about her conversation with Cynthia, how sharp she was, and what an asset she was to Perfectly Square. "We definitely need what she has to offer; I must make sure we do not lose her."

"Just watching you, I can see you have already shifted," Jim said, enjoying a bite of burrito. "Isn't it amazing how contagious moods and effective conversations can be?"

"It's funny you say that. I realized I was having an effective conversation with Cynthia in exactly the right emotion and that combination definitely created Flow for me. It was such a mutual exploration. We both felt lis-

tened to and together came up with some great ideas."
Jackie went on to share the issues they'd worked through
and the next steps they were already planning. Jim listened with a huge smile.

"My conversation with Jason was a completely different story. It was as if it started off on the wrong foot
and went downhill from there. I was committed to having
a conversation with him like I'd had with Cynthia, but
it seemed his strong, negative emotions were pulling me
down to his level, if that makes sense."

"It makes a ton of sense. Moods and emotions are
contagious. Your emotion was trumped by his stronger
emotion."

Jackie nodded. "The moment I lost my nerve and
gave into his negativity, the conversation went in exactly
the direction Jason wanted it to."

"One of my mentors told me 'the right conversation
in the wrong mood is the wrong conversation.' I've never
forgotten that."

"My conversation with Jason was definitely ineffective. Although I suppose Jason would argue it was effective because we only talked about what he wanted to,"
Jackie offered with a laugh.

"That can happen. Did you notice any missing conversations about the vision of the company?"

"Lots of them; Mark and I have been textbook examples of missing conversations in the last week. After making a good start, we've avoided taking the next step."

Jim knew this was frequently the case as people got
close to solving real issues. But he had faith that Jackie
would realize this on her own.

"The avoidance came from him at first," Jackie continued, "but then I got overwhelmed by this funk that began during my talk with Jason, so I just avoided having conversations with Mark, too. To be honest, I think they would have been ineffective anyway. I'm feeling a deep sense of resignation. It's really getting in my way."

"Sounds like you're ready to hear the last leadership tenet that wraps this all up together."

"Not sure if I am going to like hearing it."

"It won't hurt … too much."

The Woman in the Mirror

Once again Jim pulled the napkin from his notes that they had been using to draw the LeadershipFlow model. As he talked he pointed to the three tenets written on the napkin. "We've talked about organizational culture, about the need for a powerful vision that inspires others, and last time around, about the need to cultivate other leaders and teams. What's missing?" He pointed to the middle circle.

Jackie thought for a moment, before looking at Jim in confusion. "I'm not sure I'm following."

"You just said a key word: 'I.' The missing piece is the 'I,' or in your case 'you,' because—and this is the fourth tenet of Leader- shipFlow and the core of change that my former boss shared. The most difficult person you will ever have to lead is *yourself*. Self-mastery is the key to leadership and LeadershipFlow." He wrote the words "Self-Mastery" in the center of the diagram.

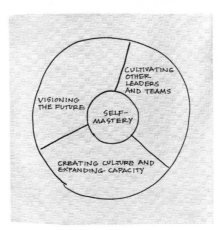

"Your leadership challenges throughout our conversations aren't Cynthia or Jason or Mark—"

"They're me. I was kind of afraid you were going to say something like that."

"It's the biggest challenge all leaders face. I faced it in every leadership situation and so do you. At its core, leading oneself is what every leader does. Think about it. You said that in the conversation with Jason your emotions stopped you from having a more effective conversation with him. Jason wasn't the issue."

"It was me."

"Same thing with Mark. If you'd shown up in an emotion and way of being that was more effective than Jason's, you both would've come away with more clarity and less unfinished business." Jim took a sip of coffee, giving Jackie a moment to process what he'd just said. "What do Mother Teresa, Gandhi, and Martin Luther King, Jr. have in common?"

"They were great human beings. Great leaders."

"They also had many millions of followers, though not one of them had a job title. Management is the authority granted to an individual by an organization. For instance, because you're part owner of Perfectly Square, you have authority granted to you to, say, fire someone from the company, correct?"

"I suppose I could, sure."

"Leadership, on the other hand, is the authority granted to an individual by his or her followers. The followers decide whom they consider to be a leader. The reasons that millions followed Dr. King, Mother Teresa, or Gandhi is that followers decided they had a future with that leader, title or no. It's no different at Perfectly Square or any organization. Employees will do things because you have management authority, but they will only follow you if they see in you a leader and a future that they want to commit to. When a leader sets the conditions for Flow, when it addresses things they care about, people follow." Jim leaned forward, intently. "To be an effective leader, you must be the leader the followers need you to be, not the leader you want to be. Those two can be very different."

They sat in silence for a moment as things sank in.

"For instance: Mark. He's not showing up as the leader the company needs, and therefore they're not motivated by him. If they are going to follow me," Jackie said with a growing sense of excitement and clarity, "I have to show up as someone they deem worthy of following. Otherwise, they'll only do what I say to avoid getting fired or in trouble. Not exactly a recipe for teamwork or collaboration or Flow or success. Just because I'm their 'boss.'"

She looked at Jim, the pieces coming together. "Just saying the word 'boss' that way shows how hollow the word can really be."

"It's a challenge for all leaders. Many are blind to how they show up, and when things go wrong, they simply place the blame on their followers."

"When in fact," Jackie added, "they should be looking to their followers to understand where they are not showing up as a leader."

"Exactly. If an employee says he or she didn't know what the leader wanted, and if the leader is open to listening, the leader can find examples of how he or she needs to lead. Not every follower needs the same thing."

"Sounds simple enough," said Jackie. "But how do you put it into action?"

"Great question. There's a discourse on leadership called ontological leadership."

"I feel like I'm back in philosophy class."

"Don't let the term throw you. It's a simple but powerful idea. Ontology is the study of being human; ontological leadership looks at leadership from this context. We've already touched on several aspects of being human."

"Conversations and moods and emotions."

"Right on. We are linguistic beings; we create our worlds with language—it's the most fundamental tool humans have. What's the first tool a baby is born with?"

For once, Jackie was stumped.

"The ability to cry, which is language. Over time, the baby learns to talk, and the more effective a person is at using language the more likely he or she will be effective in his or her pursuits." Jim spent the next ten minutes explaining what he called the speech acts, which are the foundations of conversation, and how conversations are the results of assertions, assessments, declarations, requests, offers, and promises that we make. "Still with me?"

"So far, so good," said Jackie.

"Then we're having an effective conversation," smiled Jim. "We are linguistic beings, but as you pointed out, we're also emotional beings. We cannot *not* be in a mood or emotion. Think about the word emotion: to put into motion. Moods and emotions are a predisposition to action. When something happens, we make assessments of what it means to us and then we take actions based on our moods and our emotions. Moods are a general, overall, and sometimes subtle way of looking at something."

"So it's no surprise that the funk I got into talking with Jason affected pretty much everything I've done or thought since."

"Right. Emotions are triggered by specific events. So when Jason had the conversation with you, it triggered in you a certain emotion to take action."

"It got me looking at all the negatives of the situation. Just talking to you has brought out the emotion of ambition. I can literally feel myself getting fired up again."

"We're linguistic beings and emotional beings—we are also somatic beings."

"Hello again, Philosophy one-oh-one."

Jim chuckled. "Somatic is just a fancy way of saying we have bodies. Often we think we are simply brains on a stick, and the stick simply carries us from place to place. The truth is, the body is much, much more. Have you ever met someone without a body?"

Now it was Jackie's turn to chuckle.

"Not likely, and since we have bodies, how we show up in our bodies determines what is possible, because moods and emotions live in our body. Think of Superman; how does he stand? Chest out, facing the world. Eyes up, scanning the horizon, in a mood or emotion of ambition, of can-do. That's very different from the cartoon character Sad Sack: slumped body, eyes down and sad, a mood of pity and sorrow. Both of those bodies establish what is possible. Remember you said your body started to shrink when you were in the conversation with Jason. That was not just a metaphor; it actually did."

"Yeah, I could feel my body shrinking and wanting to disappear."

As the conversation continued, Jim had Jackie try out different emotions to feel how they affected her body. She discovered this was more than an exercise; she could actually start to embody the moods they were talking about—and understand what Jim meant by leadership is an 'embodied' phenomenon. When a leader shows up in a certain body, much of the conversation is already happening.

"So we have moods and emotions, we use language, and we have bodies. What else is there?" asked Jackie.

"Two more things to think about. The first is that we have histories, and they're unique," Jim replied. "Where we grew up, our family lives, our previous jobs, our religions, our political views. All these things combine to create how we see the world. We cannot change our histories, but we can recognize that our histories determine how we see the world. It doesn't necessarily reflect the world as it really is, simply how we see it. Two people can experience the same event, yet based on their histories, walk away with wildly different perceptions.

"Kind of like how you and I see the world from the perspective of having been in the military."

"Yes. We both had positive experiences and that affects our worldview. Others might have been standing right next to us the whole time, but had negative experiences, which therefore colors their world entirely differently. And even though we both are from the military, we still see the world differently based on the other aspects of our histories that differ from one another.

"And there's one more thing that makes us human."

Still thinking about that philosophy class, Jackie wished she'd brought along something with which to take notes.

"The last thing that makes us human is our practices," continued Jim. "We're always practicing something. For instance, you practice running."

"Almost daily," Jackie said proudly.

"Because of that you are good at it, you've run marathons. Leadership is no different. You can practice having effective conversations, or you can practice ineffective conversations. You can even practice not having conversations. You can practice having moods and emotions, positive or negative. We are always practicing. We can also practice being in Flow. Effective leaders simply have better practices than others."

"So like management skills, leadership is something that can be learned."

"You bet. If you're willing to practice things like effective conversations, positive moods and emotions, and being in a body that creates those moods and emotions, you can become a more effective leader."

"I better start practicing. And the first practice is with me and how I show up."

"That's right, the woman in the mirror. All the stuff we've talked about—culture, vision, cultivating other leaders and teams—will be for naught if you are not willing to start with you, the leader. You are going to have to initiate some difficult and missing conversations. If you can't show up as a leader who can have those conversations effectively then the change cannot happen."

As much as Jackie wanted to continue the conversation, she was committed to attending a meeting. She and Jim parted ways, agreeing on a time a few weeks later. By then she planned to have had some possibly difficult, yet ultimately effective conversations with Mark, Jason, and others. As she walked to her car, she noted with some pleasure that her body was filled with a mood of ambition and possibility.

Time to Lead

As always, Jackie's conversation with Jim left her mind swirling. Between back-to-back meetings and working with Cynthia and the warehouse team on procedures designed to get a handle on shipping issues, she didn't have time to spend sorting out things as she would have liked. The day, however, was fun and invigorating and by the time she left work and was on the running trail, she was still full of energy. She used her breath to slow herself down and started to process Jim's insights. The very act reinforced in her that the body plays a very significant role in how one shows up as a leader; the conscious effort to calm down clarified her thinking.

Her first thoughts were about the conversations she wanted to have with Jason and Mark. She decided to explore the conversation with Jason first, as she knew that would shape her talk with Mark. In her initial conversation with Jason, she'd allowed the emotion of feeling inadequate set the tone, a misstep she was intent on not taking again. She explored how that negative emotion showed up in her body, her head hanging down, her frame quite literally shrinking. The debilitating story she'd told herself that she didn't earn the job or work her way up the ladder the way Jason had, caused her to tense up even during her run.

Bearing Jim's thoughts in mind, she slowed and intentionally relaxed into the run. She would have the next conversation with Jason with this body of confidence and resolve. She explored Jason's seemingly clandestine be-havior and air of entitlement that she wanted to address with him. It would be a difficult conversation for sure, but as she ran she became more and more at peace with the prospect of confronting these subjects head-on.

She then turned her thoughts to Mark. More than anything she wanted to show up in a body and emotion of caring and compassion. She wanted to have this conver-sation more as his sister than as his business partner. Visu-alizing the conversation, she started to formulate how and what she wanted to cover. They'd already brushed up against the question of whether or not Mark really want-ed to be the CEO and if so, could he commit to being the leader necessary to truly lead the company. The time had come to clearly address these issues once and for all. The conversation would be a formidable challenge, par-ticularly because Mark seemed to think everything had been resolved by their earlier conversation, blow-up, and reconciliation. To leave the matter half-resolved would be the same as having never addressed it in the first place.

By the time the run was over, Jackie was certain this was the path she should be on. She wanted to help the company succeed; regardless of the role she fulfilled, she was committed to show up as a leader.

"Now," she spoke aloud from somewhere deep inside, "it's time for me to lead!"

Just hearing the words aloud created a shift in Jackie's body. She was a leader—now it was time to go earn the title from her followers.

The Conversation with Jason

The next morning, after another great run, Jackie showed up to work more committed to the task at hand than she had been with anything she'd ever done. There was no way to know what the future might hold, and she was fully aware there would be times of overwhelming challenges and resignation. But despite the inevitable challenges that lay ahead, she was fully committed to Perfectly Square and doing all that she could do to make it a success—and this knowledge was empowering and liberating.

The previous evening, she had sent Mark and Jason each an email requesting time to get together and saw that they'd both replied; she'd see Jason at 10:30 a.m. and Mark at 2:00 p.m. She'd asked to meet Jason in the conference room to avoid being on his turf, and because her office was a bit public, it would allow for some privacy.

Jackie spent the morning finalizing the agenda for her conversation with Jason. She would explore where he fit into the organization, not in regards to his performance—after all, he had been doing great from a metrics perspective—but in terms of values. Did he really buy into the vision of the company that she was working to evolve? She knew it was a work in progress, but even so, he needed to understand that she was an owner of the company, and that even though he may not yet respect her as a leader, he did need to respect the position she occupied. She also wanted him to know that she expected his loyalty to the company to supersede his loyalty to his pocketbook. She was not 100 percent sure he was doing anything unscrupulous, but the small voice inside whispered that he was, and as a leader, she was going to address it.

When Jason strolled into the conference room five minutes late, it was apparent to Jackie that he was showing up in a body and mood of defiance, which, combined with his casual tardiness, sent the message that the conversation was going to be on his terms. Or so he thought. She took a deep breath and centered herself.

"Thanks for showing up. I want us to have a conversation about how we have conversations." He couldn't hide the shock brought on by her firmness.

"What do you mean?" he said defensively, already a little off balance.

"Our last conversation did not really live up to what I want to create here, which is an environment of mutual respect, clarity, and team work. I thought we would explore how I expect you to treat others and then you can share with me if you feel like that is something that you can commit to," she said forcefully, but calmly.

As if he had been hit on the head with a 4x4 post, it dawned on Jason that the Jackie sitting across from him was not the same person he'd walked all over in their last conversation. He sat up straight, intently listening. Jackie had caught his attention.

They spent the next thirty minutes establishing Jackie's role in the company. She made it clear that although she did not have an official title, she was one of the owners and Jason needed to understand that hierarchy. Jackie stressed that she wanted every person in the organization to show up and feel valued, but there were behaviors and actions that were non-negotiable and she wanted Jason to be clear on them.

"I also want to discuss my concerns that there are things you are doing that are ... well ... questionable." As she uttered the words, Jackie noted that Jason immediately shifted and tensed.

"I'm not accusing you of anything, but I want to be clear that the organization has certain standards of honesty and transparency. Everything we do has to be for the good of Perfectly Square, and if it isn't, it has to end." As she continued, it was obvious to both of them that Jackie was in charge, her body and emotion of ambition inarguably setting the tone. Jason said all the right things at the end of the conversation and they closed with a commitment from Jason to recommit to being a part of the team. They also committed to further conversations on a regular basis.

Afterwards, as Jackie ate lunch by herself at a small diner down the road, she reflected on what had been different this time around, what had made this conversation so effective. She showed up as the leader necessary to have the conversation, and hadn't sabotaged herself with negative emotions or a body that was contracting. She'd fulfilled her role as a leader of the company, and clearly communicated the behaviors and values she expected from him as a key player and everyone else on the team. It was effective for Jason as well. And though he might not have realized it, Jackie had shared with him what it would take for him to be a part of this team.

Whether or not he did so was up to him.

The Conversation with Mark

Jackie took a relaxed breath as she headed down the hall to Mark's office. She was proud of how she'd showed up in the conversation with Jason, but knew that she needed to have a different conversation with Mark— open and compassionate, exploring the missing conversations of how (and if) he fit into the organization as CEO, and possibly other personal issues. She knew the same determination she'd exhibited with Jason was critical; the future of the company hinged on this conversation being effective and she had to see this through to its conclusion for the sake of all involved.

She stepped into his office to find her brother in a better mood than she'd seen him in a long time; part of her hoped it was the result of their earlier conversation. She'd soon find out.

"Hey, Ace, how's my favorite sister?"

"Great, how are you?" She was encouraged by his upbeat mood.

"Great; I'm looking forward to our conversation," he replied, getting up to close the door behind her. "Lots of things I want to share."

As Jackie settled into the comfortable chair, she found herself awash in a peaceful feeling—whatever Mark had to share, however the conversation might go, it would be effective and productive.

Mark eased into the chair behind his desk. "I've been doing a lot of self-reflection since our last conversation. Just realizing the resignation and resentment I've been carrying around really opened my eyes. I really had been blind, or nearly so—viewing the world through the distorted lens of my moods. So much that they became my reality."

Jackie saw that what Mark was becoming aware of was not that he hated the company and the role of CEO, but rather that it simply was not what made him happy. Emma, Mark's longtime girlfriend, had apparently been sharing the same assessment for a long time.

"For some reason, I just didn't have the ears to hear her. Finally being able to confront my moods—to prevent them from controlling me, has already enabled me to show up differently. To be honest, I still don't know if I truly want to be CEO or not, but I know you and I are in this together and I know how passionate you are about the company. If I should step away, I know from the bottom of my heart that Perfectly Square will be in good hands."

The more Mark spoke, the more Jackie felt the Flow between them. There were many things they needed to address, but for the first time in years, they were engaged in effective conversation. For the next two hours, they talked freely, easily, and candidly about the ideas they had for the company and what the vision for Perfectly Square might look like. They each wanted to keep all the good things that their father had created while adding new ideas and practices to create Flow in the organization that would guide them to the bright future they both could see. Those would be future conversations.

For now Jackie was overcome with joy and satisfaction that, finally, they were effectively talking.

What's Next — The Fifth Burrito

The next few weeks flew by for Jackie as she continued to find Flow in herself and the organization. She found conversations everywhere and practiced showing up in them, enabling everyone involved to participate in a powerful, meaningful way. By the time her next breakfast with Jim rolled around, she had a thousand things to share. When Jim stepped through the door at precisely 8:00 a.m., he found Jackie and breakfast waiting.

"Wow, who is that radiating energy?" he smiled as he sat across from her.

"Just a simple woodworking supply store owner who loves what she does."

"I like the sound of that," Jim replied and they both dove into the still steaming burritos.

"I have had some great conversations," Jackie said between bites. She filled Jim in on how the conversations with both Jason and Mark were determined by the way she showed up in her body, her moods and emotions, and how she used language. She still needed lots of practice, but having scratched the surface, was excited about what lay ahead.

"I'm truly seeing how it all fits together. As you said, the culture we have is one-hundred percent perfect to get the results we are getting. And two of the most important things shaping that culture are the nature of our conversations, and our individual and collective moods and emotions. If we want to change the culture, we need to be clear on our vision for the future—the necessary conversations, moods, and emotions that will help build it—ultimately creating Flow. We need effective and high-functioning leaders and teams committed to the vision to bring it alive, and at the root of it all is self-mastery." She smiled at her mentor. "The most difficult person I'll ever have to lead is myself. And the best way to do that is, every day, to purposefully use language and master my moods, emotions, and body. That's what will determine whether others will follow me as a leader and find Flow."

"You're getting it," said Jim, with more than a hint of pride. "Now the fun begins. Start building an organization that will thrive in the future."

"Only if we keep having coffee and burritos every step of the way."

"Deal," Jim replied with a grin.

Epilogue | A Year Later

Jackie was unaware of the significance of the date but when she arrived at work she found a small envelope next to a rather large, flat, wrapped package adorned with a bow. Filled with curiosity, she gently opened the envelope.

One year ago my sister came back home to help with the family business. Little did I know the gift she would give me. Thanks and I love you,

Your brother, THE ARTIST—off finding Flow,
Mark

She then delicately removed the bow and wrapping paper to reveal something that nearly took her breath away. A beautiful oil painting of a sparkling stream meandering through slick, gray, mossy rocks—dappled by sunlight, suffused in subtle hues of blue, tourmaline, and emerald.

Flow.

In the corner she found the nearly invisible initials: "M.A." She gently traced them with her finger, filled with love and gratitude. Flow indeed.

So much had happened in the past year. She and Mark had the pleasure of working side by side for nearly six months, one of the most productive and fulfilling times of her life. They'd had amazing conversations about everything from the vision for the company to what Mark really wanted to do with his life. In the end, his desire to be an artist was too great, so he opened a small studio not far from the store. Many times as Jackie drove home from another long day in the office, she saw the studio lights burning into the night and smiled at the thought of her brother immersed in his work, completely oblivious to the passage of time. He was still very involved with the company, a valuable sounding board for Jackie in her new role as CEO. He even dropped by occasionally and helped out with an inventory or a big sales event; he was always ready with a creative idea to help solve an issue with marketing or a concern about the future of the company.

There had also been personnel changes. Jason Shumway departed about two months after he and Jackie had their conversation. There was never anything conclusive about whether or not he was doing anything unscrupulous, but Jackie showing up as a leader with clarity regarding behaviors she expected motivated him to find employment elsewhere. Jackie created the role of Operations Manager and the obvious choice was Cynthia, whose energy and attitude were rivaled only by Jackie's. She had really rolled up her sleeves and solved many of the internal issues the company faced. There were still issues to work on, but as Cynthia liked to say, "I *get* to work on them, I don't *have* to work on them." Jackie and Cynthia continued to have effective conversations on a regular basis, which were invariably among the highlights of Jackie's day. People like Patrick were given opportunities to thrive in positions that challenged them. The team was engaged, each person bringing his or her best every day and as a result, Perfectly Square had its best year ever.

Jackie also created a cross-functional team to work on the company's vision and a five-year plan to achieve it. Some of the members of the team were even old Table Saw Mafia members, who, because of the effective conversations of leaders like Jackie and Cynthia, now saw a powerful future for the organization. Jackie was at the center of a group not afraid to share thoughts, the very embodiment of an environment in which Flow lives.

Jim Catlett, not one to miss out, joined the team as the Chief Culture Officer, helping to make sure that the team never lost its focus on finding Flow and having fun.

Jackie loved every minute as CEO. She awoke every morning knowing that the day's outcome would be determined by the conversations and the emotions she embodied in herself and instilled in others.

Post Script

This book is an amalgamation of forty years of studying leadership. It all started when I was eight-years-old and dove into Omar Bradley's autobiography, *A Soldier's Story*. I have been hesitant to write a book for two reasons. The first being that it has taken me years to really have a fundamental understanding of leadership, and the second, a concern about how I could share my perspectives on this topic in a manner that did not sound like a graduate level dissertation. The first reason eventually took care of itself, having spent twenty-two plus years as a leader in the military, almost that amount of time as an owner of a small consulting firm, and as an expert coach and consultant in the study of leadership. The second was taken care of by finding a way to write a narrative drawing on my real experiences.

The characters and the story line in this book are somewhat true. As I set out to explain LeadershipFlow I thought of all of the leaders and organizations I have been a part of. Each added to the story. Some of the characters are based on actual leaders I have had the pleasure (and challenge) of working with and for in the past. The organizations are ones that I have seen and been deeply immersed in. As is said on TV, the characters and organizations' names and industries have been changed to protect the innocent.

The concept of LeadershipFlow is based on my experience of being in many different organizations as a coach and consultant, from my experience of being a leader in the military, and as a small business owner. As I worked with the many organizations I found there were four statements that I would repeat to my coaching clients and myself:

"The culture you have is one-hundred percent perfect to get the results you are currently getting." (Creating Culture and Expanding Capacity)

"There are two fundamental things a leader must do: First, create a vision that others are committed to." (Visioning the Future)

"Second, create other leaders and teams committed to that vision." (Cultivating other Leaders and Teams)

"The most difficult person you will ever have to lead is yourself." (Self-Mastery)

My study of leadership has been greatly influenced by an emerging field called ontological coaching, which looks at what it means to been human, and from there, how to show up as a leader. As a student of this field I have been influenced by teachers such as Julio Olalla, Dr. Fernando Flores, Bob Dunham, and Dr. Richard Strozzi-Heckler, and countless other teachers and coaches. Many of the ideas presented in this book have been generated and influenced by these teachers' thinking and writings. I do not claim to be the originator of the ideas or concepts, but rather wish to give all of my teachers and their teachers the credit.

Ontological coaching looks at how we, as humans, observe the world. Specifically, how our use of language, our moods and emotions, and our bodies, combine to shape how we see the world. This understanding allows us to see leadership at a 'cellular' level and is a very powerful lens through which to explore leadership.

Three years ago I was introduced to the concept of Flow, and the neuroscience of peak human performance. The concept was really brought alive by Mihaly Csikszentmihalyi, (Me-High Chick-Sent-Me-High) considered the 'Godfather' of Flow in the '70s, with his studies of happiness. The concept is being studied extensively now, and in my case, author Steven Kotler's book, *The Rise of Superman*, greatly influenced how I see Flow. And what I saw blew my mind; I had discovered the Holy Grail of Leadership. If a leader could find and tap Flow, then the rest would take care of itself.

LeadershipFlow, then, is bringing out the best in individuals and organizations by tapping Flow through embodied leadership behaviors, which can be learned and practiced. It is the continual intersection of four principles: self-mastery, visioning the future, cultivating other leaders and teams, and creating culture and expanding capacity.

It is from this foundation that this book was written.

Some Frequently Asked Questions

In my travels and conversations (hopefully, mostly effective), many clients and fellow leaders have shared their questions with me. Here are some common ones and my thoughts on them.

1. Can Flow be maintained for an extended period of time or does it come and go?

Flow is not an eternal destination; rather we, as humans, ebb in an out of Flow. Research is showing that Flow follows a predictable cycle. First, there must be a struggle where our skills are being pushed to their limits by a challenge. At some point we let go, which is when Flow shows up. The last stage is recovery. Those who find Flow more often are ones who continually push themselves to the limit of their skills and then let go and get into the Flow. These people also allow themselves to effectively recover.

2. Is Flow eternal within an organization or is decay and the need to reinvent inevitable?

The status quo will eventually lead to Flow states diminishing. Remember that there must be challenges, which continually push up against an organization's skills and abilities. Think of a heavily bureaucratic or monopoly type organization. After a while, because of the rote nature of the organization, individuals will not feel challenged or inspired, so eventually Flow will ebb. Growth and change are necessary for Flow to show up.

3. If you're not authentically feeling positive emotions, can faking it still bear results?

When I hear a question like this, I start to explore what mood or emotions the person asking the question is in when the question is asked. If you find that you are not in positive moods and emotions, then your practice becomes an exploration of your current state and what it would take for you to shift and see the challenge from a mood or emotion that would yield different results. This is at the core of the ontological perspective: how you observe the world determines what conversations are possible. This is also at the core of LeadershipFlow: Self-Mastery.

4. Do these concepts of having conversations apply if you are not in position of power?

The premise of effective conversations is not tied to roles of authority. From my perspective, any person is a leader and any person can have effective conversations. Chances are you are already having many effective conversations. The simple act of buying a pair of shoes requires an effective conversation. Where many leaders are challenged with effective conversations is where they have strong negative moods and emotions. These can be worked through practice.

5. What are the keys to recognizing a missing conversation?

The best way to determine a missing conversation is to explore where you, as a leader, are dissatisfied. Where you are not getting the results you expect, or others are not following through like you feel they should, most likely means there has not been an effective conversation. Moods and emotions are a way your body lets you know that there are some missing conversations. Frustrated that your partner did not do something? Make a more effective request.

6. How long does it take to be working on self-mastery before it becomes more or less automatic?

Self-mastery is a life-long journey. Remember, to create Flow it is necessary to be challenged. Think back to when you were a kid; something as simple as riding a bike was a challenge. Through practice, the more you rode your bike the better you got. At some point, most of us stop riding bikes for fun because we move on to other activities that are more challenging. Rare is the person who continues to grow. Self-mastery must be a life-long pursuit ...

7. The book references moods and emotions throughout. Are they same thing?

Although they may seem the same, there are differences between moods and emotions. Emotions are physiological responses that are triggered by an event, whereas moods are a mental state that shapes how someone sees his or her world. As an example, say you are driving down the road and thinking about how lucky you are to have the life you have (mood). All of a sudden your car is in a minor fender bender. The fender bender can trigger various emotions in you such as anger at the other driver or gratitude that no one is hurt. Both of those emotions are caused by the event (the fender bender), and will likely dissipate over time. However, they can become moods if they stay and influence how you see other events in your life.

8. How do you bring LeadershipFlow alive in organizations?

On the simplest level, you have to practice it, and guess what you practice? Effective conversations, and effective moods and emotions, among other things. When we go into an organization to help them become higher performing we generally do two things. First, we spend a lot of time with the clients exploring how they have conversations and what moods they are in. (Creating Culture and Expanding Capacity). We then start looking at what is their vision of the future (Visioning the Future). We do this through what we call Leadership Conversations where we bring the leaders and teams together (Cultivating Other Leaders and Teams) and we explore what they, as an organization, need to do to create their future. This is done with every leader, exploring how they are showing up as leaders (Self-Mastery) and what they and others need to commit to in order to create their future. In effect we practice the conversations and moods/emotions necessary to create the future.

Second, we spend lots of time in coaching conversations both with individuals and teams to reinforce the learning of new distinctions and help individuals become the leaders necessary to create and sustain the change. This is done through transactional coaching (how to get from A to B) all the way to transformational coaching (how to shift how one is showing up as a leader).

9. What resources do you recommend for more information on the science of Flow or Ontological Coaching?

We have set up a landing page at www.croftandcompany.com/leadershipflow/resources, which will share many of the references and resources for you and your organization to explore these concepts further.

Notes

This book would not be possible without the generative/ontological discourse, which is at the root of the story. The discourse is much bigger than one person and many have added to the collective wisdom. I do wish to point out the following specific items.

Bob Dunham, founder of the Institute of Generative Leadership contributed much to this discourse, in particular:

From his paper *The Generative Foundations of Action in Organizations: Speaking and Listening,* International Journal of Coaching in Organizations, Volume 7, issue 2, 2009.

–Page 39—Effective, Ineffective and Missing Conversations

–Page 50—"I will" exercise.

–Page 96—Definition of Leadership and Management—From the Coaching Excellence in Organizations (CEO) program.

The quote, "The right conversation in the wrong mood is the wrong conversation," page 92 has been attributed to Julio Olalla.